HEART POLITICS

Heart Politics

by

Fran Peavey

with Myra Levy and Charles Varon

Illustrations by Leonard Rifas

new society publishers

ISBN: 0-86571-076-7 hardcover; 0-86571-077-5 paperback
Printed in the United States

Cover design by Brian Prendergast
Book design by Myra Levy and Nina Huizinga

New Society Publishers is a project of New Society Educational
Foundation and a collective of Movement for a New Society. New
Society Educational Foundation is a non-profit, tax-exempt public
foundation. Movement for a New Society is a network of small
groups and individuals working for fundamental social change through
nonviolent action. To learn more about MNS write: Movement for
a New Society, 4722 Baltimore Avenue, Philadelphia, PA 19143.
Opinions expressed in this book do not necessarily represent positions
of either New Society Educational Foundation or Movement for a
New Society.

Foreword

What gives me hope?

Often I am asked this question. In a world in which solid ground for hope seems to diminish by the day, the only kind of hope many people can imagine is a blind faith that somehow everything will work out—a denial of the evil that appears to be gaining on us.

But I am convinced that there is such a thing as "honest hope," hope that is constructed not upon denial, simplistic formulas, or otherworldly dreams.

Honest hope derives from a belief that positive change is possible in the world. And we will only believe this if we experience ourselves changing. The key is *risk,* doing that which we thought we could not do.

Fran Peavey has chosen precisely this path to honest hope. She has taken risks that many of us could never even imagine. *Heart Politics* is profoundly unsettling. It is disturbing because in it we live through her many risks—of physical harm, of humiliation, of social ostracism. She doesn't spare us the discomfort she feels. So, in some small sense, reading this book we risk, too. We risk having many of our assumptions and self-protective shields challenged.

Believing in the possibility of real change—transformative change of our distressed world—means being willing to cultivate in our adult lives the shameless impudence of children—but a shamelessness not from innocence, and an impudence not from a mere automatic rejection of authority. Rather I mean a willingness to look with fresh eyes, to refuse to take as givens the shoulds and should-nots handed down to us, and, most of all, a determination to follow through on the logical moral consequences of what we learn. Fran Peavey is shamelessly impudent!

The challenge of *Heart Politics* is that it doesn't ask for our approval. It doesn't try to convince us that Fran's choices are noble, or *the* way to change the world. It doesn't tell us which risks to take. Rather, *Heart Politics* challenges us to look at our own choices with fresh eyes and ask: Of what am *I* capable that I thought perhaps I did not have the courage to attempt?

Frances Moore Lappé

Table of Contents

Introduction

IN COLLEGE, I had a recurrent nightmare that I was being pursued by people wielding picket signs. One sign said "Democrat," another "Republican," another "Communist." There was one sign in favor of the death penalty and another against. All the different points of view on issues that were controversial to me were represented, and the people chasing me were trying to hit me over the head with these signs.

Looking back at the twenty years since then, I see that my life's work has been a search for effective ways to bring about change without clobbering people with my ideas. *Heart Politics* tells some of the stories of that search.

I write as one four–billionth of the human species, as an American living in the twentieth century, as an ordinary person who has always had to work for a living. Although this book is based on my experiences, it is not an autobiography. The focus is not my life but the conclusions I have drawn from it and the questions my experience has led me to ask.

This book prescribes no specific set of actions or objectives. Rather, it suggests a way of looking at the world and being guided through it by our hearts and minds in concert. It explores a new way of understanding ourselves in relation to the world around us. It is about how we grapple with the complex and perplexing questions of our time, how we build connections with people whose lives are different from ours, and how we write our own parts in the collaborative drama of history.

Fran Peavey
San Francisco, April 1985

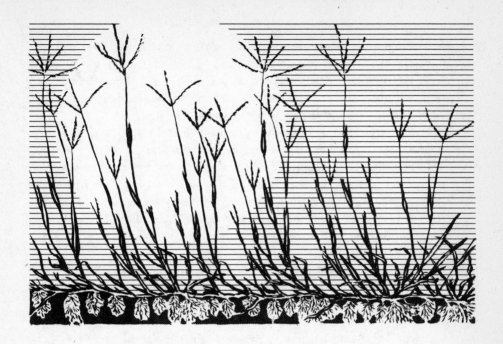

1 | *Connectedness*

HUMAN BEINGS are a lot like crabgrass. Each blade of crabgrass sticks up into the air, appearing to be a plant all by itself. But when you try to pull it up, you discover that all the blades of crabgrass in a particular piece of lawn share the same roots and the same nourishment system. Those of us brought up in the Western tradition are taught to think of ourselves as separate and distinct creatures with individual personalities and independent nourishment systems. But I think the crabgrass image is a more accurate description of our condition. Human beings may appear to be separate, but our connections are deep and we are inseparable.

1

MY DAD USED TO have us pick spuds in the fall with the Mexican farmworkers, "to keep us humble." And I remember being disgusted with the Mexicans when they would pee in the field. Why didn't they just go into the farm owner's house the way I did? They must be backward, primitive people who didn't use toilets.

Still, I argued with those in my family who said Mexicans were inferior. My brother and sister would call you a Mexican when you did something really stupid. That's not right, I used to say, they're just people like all the rest of us. But if you are washed over with any attitude for a long time, even if you object to it, some of it seeps into your skin and becomes part of you. Years later I was to discover shadows of that prejudice in myself.

During my first year of teaching, at Roosevelt Junior High School in San Francisco, there was a student named Roberto who always irritated me. One day he asked, "Miss Peavey, do you think it has anything to do with the fact that you don't like Mexicans?" I was stunned. Of course I defended myself against his accusation, but over time I came to think that he was right.

About ten years later, I went to Mexico during my Christmas vacation to lead several counseling workshops. People usually started telling me their problems in English, but when they got really absorbed, they switched to Spanish. Since I didn't speak Spanish, I had to learn to listen closely to the emotional tone of what they were saying. I was surprised at how much I could understand.

One day I took a tourist trip by private car. When I tried to sit in the front seat to get a better view, the driver asked me to move to the back. This turned out to be a matter of class: lower class people were expected to sit in front, and rich Americans in back. Soon a poor woman carrying a baby got in and sat next to the driver. She didn't speak much English. After driving awhile we stopped for refreshments, and when I got back to the car, the woman was sitting there crying. I didn't know what to do—our cultures were so different. So I just tapped her on the shoulder and said, "Is there something wrong, Señora?" She turned around and looked at me. Then she got out of the car, sat down next to me, and started telling me her story.

It seems that she had given birth to thirteen children, and only two were still living—a six-year-old son and this little baby. Now the baby was very sick. She was afraid he was going to die, and she was taking him to the children's hospital in Mexico City. She told me the story mostly in Spanish. I couldn't follow the details, but as she cried I put my arm around her and listened, and I understood the gist of what she was saying.

When the baby started crying, the woman stiffened and tried to get him to quiet down. I said, "No, no, the baby's trying to get well. He's telling you how hard it is for him right now. It's all right for the baby to cry." I held the crying baby in one arm and his mother in the other, and just paid attention. As we were getting close to Mexico City, she said, "It took me two days to find the money to come here, so I didn't have time to take the baby to have the priest bless him. Would you bless the baby?" At first I was utterly embarrassed. I didn't know anything about baby-blessing! But my second thought was: After all, what is a blessing? Blessing is saying, "All of the power and love that I am in touch with I give open-heartedly to you."

I started talking to the little baby—about how hard it must be, but that life was really worth it; that there were people all around the world who would love him if he could just grow up, if he would just hang on. But if he couldn't we would all understand. I started crying too, feeling how hard the baby's life was. Maybe he didn't have enough food, maybe his mother couldn't give him enough milk. And he was very sick—his skin looked green and yellow. I kept thinking: I know so many people who would love this baby. Remembering all the friends I loved in San Francisco, I thought: Their love extends to you, little one. The only reason they don't love you is that they don't know you yet. They would love you if they were here; since I'm here, I represent them and pass their love to you. It seemed like a reasonable blessing to me.

When we reached Mexico City I got her a taxi and paid the fare so she could hurry off to the hospital. I had a stamped postcard in my pocket, and I wrote my name and address on it and said, "I want you to send this to me and tell me how the little one turns out." She said she couldn't write. I said, "Well, you must find a way, because I really care about this situation." About two weeks later the postcard arrived. "Fernando is well, we are home from the hospital. Thank you very much. May God bless you. Rosa Rosales, by her sister's hand. P.S. Please visit us the next time you come to San José Purua."

AS A SOPHOMORE in high school, I attended a Presbyterian conference in Iowa with young people from all over the country. My roommates there were two black girls from the South. This was my first contact with Southerners, not to mention black Southerners. All I knew about relations between whites and blacks in the South was that for some baffling reason, when confronted with blacks, white people became vicious, yelled hateful things, and formed lynching parties. I was relieved when that was not my response.

I could tell there were some real cultural differences when we all got together in our room. Timidly I asked a few questions, but mostly I watched and listened. I was surprised and pleased that we could be cordial with each other. It gave me hope that someday, if necessary, I could get along with "Negroes."

Some months later, reading *Time* magazine, I saw a picture of one of my conference roommates trying to enroll in high school. She was tall and skinny and was wearing a plaid dress. Someone was sticking fingers up behind her head to indicate that she had horns. I remember feeling cold with fear for her, and at the same time admiring her courage. She was making history.

From my experience with her, I had learned that being white didn't automatically mean one had to behave in an uncivil way to black people. It was puzzling to me that other white people acted that way.

Roosevelt Junior High was halfway between Pacific Heights—a relatively rich white neighborhood—and the Fillmore district—mainly a black neighborhood, especially then. Roughly a third of my students at Roosevelt were black.

About the second week of school, I realized that I didn't know anything about being black. It was 1963, and black history hadn't been "discovered" yet. So I went to the local NAACP chapter and said, "I'm teaching your children, and I don't have any idea what their life experience is." I asked them to teach me about black history and the worldview of black kids. I had a lot of questions.

So after school once a week, I went for my "black lessons." I hoped my fellow teachers wouldn't find out about what I was doing—it was an admission of my naiveté about black culture, and teachers aren't supposed to be naive. I wondered about the other white teachers at Roosevelt: did they all know about black life?

My tutors, black NAACP volunteers, took me around to meet people in the neighborhood. I lived on the edge of the Fillmore district, so I also met black people in the grocery store and became part of the community, a little bit anyway.

My tutors took me to people's homes, workplaces, and churches. They would introduce me as the teacher from Roosevelt who wanted to learn about the black community. I noticed that people would warm up and talk in a way that they wouldn't if my tutor weren't there. I'd ask them what their lives were like, what they wanted their children to learn, how school had been for them, how those who were parents felt when they visited their children's schools for open house night. They pinned a lot of their hopes for their kids on the school but felt it to be an alien institution—one where many had never felt at home. Even now, many felt intimidated by their children's teachers.

It was a great relief to be able to ask the questions that came up for me during the school week, especially in a situation where people valued my asking. One lesson was at a beauty parlor. I learned about the techniques for "processing" black people's hair. So one day when I came into class with a permanent and the kids said, "Oh look, Miss Peavey's got her hair processed," I could respond intelligently and openly about the different ways each race deals with its hair aspirations.

One week I asked why so many black men were always standing on the street in the neighborhood. My tutor took me to visit with a few of them. Most didn't have jobs, I learned. They liked being outside, where they could see their friends and catch up on news. The streetcorner was their office, their meeting place. And, contrary to my assumption, few men stayed on the street all day long. Most spent a few hours and then moved on.

Because I was a science teacher, I made a point of meeting with doctors and technicians who told me about getting their education in the sciences and described the difficulties of attaining their positions. I remember one inhalation therapist who told me that until recently he had never heard of any famous black scientists besides George

Washington Carver. He also told me how hard it had been for him to get his license, even though he had been working in the field for several years. He laid the blame on himself and asserted that he would be able to succeed through hard work. After we left, my tutor explained that if I hadn't been there, the therapist might have pointed to racial discrimination as the key obstacle in his professional career. But, my guide told me, it is frightening for black people to let whites see the anger and vulnerability they feel when faced with discrimination.

I've always been grateful to my tutors for being patient with me and for pointing out when my assumptions were based on ignorance or prejudice. For instance, I would frequently correct my black students' grammar. They would say "we was" or "I ain't gonna do that no more"—things like that. I noticed these errors were consistent, so I asked one of my tutors, "Why do they keep making the same mistakes?" She explained that just as American English is different from British English, black English is different from white English. African languages had their own syntax, she explained, and some of it may have been retained. She said that while most black parents would appreciate my sharing white English with their children (so they could have a better chance at economic success), I should be careful not to *put down* black kids for the way they spoke, or to consider it wrong. That might communicate that it was wrong to be black.

I adopted a rule in those lessons that I have found useful many times since. I do not defend myself when someone points out an oppressive attitude or racist remark of mine. What I've said may be well-intended, but that isn't really relevant when it has hurt another person.

Of course, sometimes I felt unfairly accused or misunderstood, and often I felt confused, but I was learning. It was necessary to go through feelings like those in order to become a firm ally of black people.

In 1966 race riots flared up in San Francisco. I still lived on the edge of the Fillmore district, although I wasn't teaching at Roosevelt anymore. One evening I heard pebbles hitting my window. I looked out and saw people in the street shouting and jeering. One of them yelled, "We want you down here! We want you down here, Miss

Peavey!" It was a group of about twenty black kids, most of them former students of mine. And they were wired. I was scared to go downstairs—it felt like walking into a mob. Some friends were visiting me, and I told them, "Turn off the lights. When I go down there, stand at the window and watch. If I run into trouble, call the police." Then I went downstairs, keeping my hands out of my pockets so the kids would realize I was totally defenseless. My friends were watching from the window. I said to the kids, "Why don't you come on upstairs?" So up they came, while my friends stayed in the kitchen. We were scared.

I sat until about midnight, listening. The kids recounted their day's activities: rioting, breaking windows, turning cars over, and getting even with the honkies, the charlies who had been bugging them for years. They told of smashing the window of a store whose owner had always treated them badly, and stealing some liquor. They were proud to be evening things out for their people. I had never felt such a sense of power in a group of people.

My friends in the kitchen started making cookies—three people in my tiny kitchen made different cookie recipes for hours. They kept an ear to the door, listening to the kids' stories. I kept bringing the cookies in. I felt very privileged to be listening to those kids. I began to realize how separated, how isolated, we had been from each other and what the effects of that isolation had been on them.

My grandmother Carpenter used to say to me it would break her heart if I married a black man. We would have little arguments, but nobody could ever argue much with my grandmother because she was so beloved. And since my marriage to a black man wasn't imminent, it didn't seem necessary to fight about it. Like me, she had never really known any black people.

One year she came from Idaho to visit me in San Francisco. There was a little grocery store on my corner that had a real community feeling. A bunch of us always stopped in around 5:00 P.M.: the garbage man, the Deputy, Jimmy and Louie (the two Chinese guys who ran the store), and me—I was called Teach. We stood around and kibbitzed every night. If you didn't come by for a couple of days they would send somebody to see if you were all right, and if you were sick they'd send groceries over. It felt like our grocery store. If there was a rush of business, we'd go back and bag groceries for Jimmy and Louie, and we all had charge accounts even though officially charge accounts weren't allowed.

Deputy, a tall, attractive black man of forty-five or fifty, was behind the counter the day I walked in and announced I wanted to introduce my grandmother. In a second he was in front of us, saying, "I want to give your grandmother a big kiss." My heart stopped. What if my grandmother wasn't gracious? What if she hurt Deputy's feelings? While my heart was hovering there, refusing to beat, my grandmother gave Deputy a big kiss.

Later, when we went outside, I said to her, "I was kind of surprised, because I know how you feel about black people." She answered, "Why Frances, I'm sure any friend of yours must be a very fine person."

It occurred to me then that it's easier to be prejudiced against people you've never met. Fear and hatred can thrive in the abstract. But most of us, if given a protected situation and a personal connection to the people we thought we feared or hated, will come through as compassionate human beings. Although my grandmother had openly prejudiced attitudes, her human decency overcame those attitudes for a moment.

Later in my work I began to think of connectedness as a political principle. Even some of our seemingly noblest efforts have a kind of delusion at the center because they lack heart. If we aren't connected to the people we think we're fighting for, there's an emptiness, a coldness at the center. It's the same coldness that's at the heart of prejudice—the coldness of separation.

BEFORE COMING TO SAN FRANCISCO, I'd never heard about gay people. My response upon hearing of the phenomenon of people being attracted to people of their own gender was: Well, it's logical. If you flip two coins, sometimes they'll be heads and heads, sometimes tails and tails, and sometimes heads and tails. One shouldn't expect that men will love only women, or women love only men. I saw homosexuality as a statistical imperative. The person I said this to couldn't figure out how to begin to disabuse me of this weird idea.

Homosexuality became an issue for me when I was working at San Francisco State, supervising student teachers. It was 1971, before most heterosexuals were particularly aware of gay people. One of my student teachers came to me with a problem: she had received a love letter from one of her students—a girl.

I knew I was out of my depth. So I told her the only thing I really knew about how to learn in such a situation: "When you're wondering about a group of people who are different from you, find someone from that group and ask them to teach you." After making a few phone calls, we found two lesbians to meet with us. They told us what it was like to be gay. Homosexuals were a minority even in their own families and found it difficult to find allies with whom they could explore their feelings without being ostracized. To be accepted, most had to maintain the pretense of being heterosexual. This made them feel dishonest and resulted in unstable connections with other people.

Soon after this meeting, I offered a weekend workshop for teachers on sex education. It included a panel of teenagers, some heterosexual and some gay, talking about what school was like for them. The gay kids described their experiences: in school, they were isolated and lonely, without any good role models. Fellow students, as well as teachers, were always teasing them. One guy told of developing a tough demeanor as a defense. Others complained of feeling excluded from social events, like dances, that were biased toward heterosexuals. They felt they had to play games with their identities, and for years lived in fear of having their secret discovered.

After the workshop, many teachers who had attended began inviting gay speakers to their high school sex education classes. In stepping forward as allies of gay people, we found ourselves in a controversial position. Soon my students were getting fired all over the Bay Area.

WITH EACH NEW CONNECTION I made, I felt a little less confused and lonely, and a little more secure. Usually this security was a general feeling, but there were times it became more tangible. One night as I walked to my car, a black man about my age pulled a knife on me. Just then another guy came up behind him and said, "Hey, man, that's my teacher, Miss Peavey. You leave her alone." There stood Percy, one of my black students from Roosevelt, looking out for me.

2 | Seeds

WHEN I WAS YOUNG, I thought Twin Falls, Idaho, must be the hub of the world, like Rome in ancient times. My grandfather Carpenter used to say, "You can get anywhere from Twin Falls. All the roads to the rest of the world come through here." But people rarely seemed to take those roads that led to the rest of the world. As I grew up, I didn't meet many people whose ideas or backgrounds were much different from my parents'. Our daily newspaper focused on local events and didn't pay much attention to international news.

Now, finding myself in the streets of Jerusalem or New Delhi, I think: What an unlikely thing! Here are my Idaho feet walking

11

on these streets. It's astonishing. Standing on a stage in Los Angeles or Liverpool performing comedy, or sitting in jail after a civil disobedience action, I wonder how I've come so far from where I was "supposed to be."

I was supposed to marry an Idahoan. A farmer would have been acceptable but a businessman or a professional was preferable. I was suppposed to have kids and probably be a schoolteacher, because if something were to happen to my husband I should be prepared to take care of my family. Even when I was a kid, my mother could tell that I had a natural talent for teaching: after learning how to read I came home and taught my younger brother and sister.

My parents expected me to go to college and get a bachelor's degree—but doctoral work? They wouldn't have been prepared for the fact that I'm happy as a fat, imperfect person who can't balance her checkbook. I don't derive my livelihood or direction from a larger institution. I don't go to the beauty parlor every week to have my hair done. I was expected to tend a very small plot: a family, neighbors, a classroom of kids. That would have been the scope of my heart and my mind. Instead, I find myself treating countries all over the world as "neighboring plots" and carrying the people of those countries in my heart and mind. I find myself trying to integrate the personal and the global in my life.

MY GRANDPARENTS on both sides of the family came west to Idaho before the turn of the century. Some came by covered wagon. My ancestors homesteaded, got established, and eventually prospered. The pioneer experience is part of our family identity.

My father was a successful insurance salesman who also supervised a number of farms in the area for a Dutch land company. My mother, a former schoolteacher, stayed home and raised five children. Our life was stable and comfortable.

The Peavey family is prominent in Idaho. My father's parents were among the earliest settlers in Twin Falls, and Peaveys have always had a reputation for being civic-minded. Growing up, I learned that there were certain things that Peaveys didn't do. Other people could shout, call attention to themselves, go barefoot in public, go downtown in pants instead of a skirt—but not us. My mother, a Carpenter, was proud to marry a Peavey, and she was eager to promulgate those standards.

WE FLEW THE FLAG on patriotic holidays. At our summer cabin
in Idaho's beautiful Stanley Basin, we put the flag up every day—
that was the sign we were home. On the Fourth of July, everyone
from the cabins around Pettit Lake gathered at the flagpole. All the
children sang songs like "My Country 'Tis of Thee" and the Idaho
state anthem, and recited the pledge of allegiance. Elmer
Hollingsworth, the self-appointed mayor of Pettit Lake, gave a
speech. Our parents spoke, too, about settling the West and what
America meant. They told us the United States was a strong, great
country, full of free, friendly, hard-working people. We were instructed
to take care of our country and to live in a way that would make
our country proud. As I recall, that meant voting, not littering,
and not starting forest fires. Our obligation to go to war was mentioned
only obliquely, as my grandmother Peavey was a pacifist. After the
speeches we ate brunch, and in the evening we played baseball among
the pine trees. There was a barbecue supper, and then we shot
fireworks over the lake. It was a beautiful and exciting day, one of
the best of the year.

In history and civics classes I believed exactly what I was taught:
that in this country, the people rule. Like so many others who go
through the U.S. educational system, I became a great idealist.

Every four years my father would take us to the polls. I remember
going there with him in the evening; he would squat down next to
me and say in a hushed voice, "This is the way we elect the President.
This is the way the people run the country." You had to be quiet
at the polls—no running around. It was almost a sacred place.

My family was staunchly Republican and prominent in the local
party. Dad was treasurer of the state Republican committee. Aunt
Mary was married to U.S. Senator C. Waylan Brooks; and after his
death, she was chairwoman of the Republican National Committee.
Later, under President Nixon, she ran the U.S. Mint.

LIFE WAS MANAGEABLE in Twin Falls. We knew our neighbors, our
policemen, the schoolteachers, the superintendent of schools. Soon
after getting my driver's license, I made an illegal left turn in town
and was ticketed for it. I went to pay the fine, and there was Judge
Pumphreys. He said to me, "Frances, it's a great disappointment

to me to have you appear in court before me. I remember when you were a little girl and you had a pink dress . . ." He went on for a while in this vein, and then said that I would either have to spend a night in jail or pay thirteen dollars "of money you've earned yourself." (I naively chose the jail time, thinking it more attractive than going home to face my parents. Of course my parents found out, and I learned that spending time in jail is an offense far worse than making an illegal left turn.)

Given my family's social position, it wasn't hard to get things done. When our high school was being moved to a new building, my grandmother Peavey decided that the now-separate junior high school should be named for Vera O'Leary, the retired long-time principal. My dad said he would take care of it. So he talked to the appropriate friends, and the school board agreed to name it O'Leary Junior High School. My grandmother was furious! The name they had chosen would appear to be honoring a man. So she and my dad went to the next school board meeting and got the name changed to *Vera* O'Leary Junior High School.

My Sunday school teacher was also the local FBI man and wore his gun to class. I had read about the FBI in books and in *Time* magazine, and I tried to imagine what his life was like, chasing criminals in Twin Falls. Were there really criminals there just like in New York City? It was something special to have our own FBI man, keeping our part of the nation secure.

I OWE SOME OF MY CURIOSITY about ideas to my grandmother Peavey. She lived near us in Twin Falls, and we visited her frequently. Grams was always old, even when I was young. Her family had left Wisconsin when she was a child, traveling around Cape Horn in South America to California. She was one of the first women graduate students at Stanford University, where she studied history. A voracious reader, Grams always kept current on the ideas that were being discussed in the *New Yorker* and the *Atlantic*. She once recounted some advice from her mother: when traveling by stagecoach, a woman could ward off unwanted advances from men by carrying an *Atlantic Monthly* and appearing to be an intellectual.

When we were in elementary school, Grams began inviting her grandchildren and our best friends over for afternoon tea parties. There would usually be three of us at each party, and the first one to ask "Can I pour?" would assume that prized responsibility. Then we bid for the identities we were to assume for the duration of the tea. Mrs. Gotrocks was my favorite. There were also Mrs. Smythe and Mrs. Elderfinger.

Tea was served, usually on the patio, and Grams would pose a question for our consideration. It might be about electoral politics, the quality of the schools, our thoughts about the future, our philosophy of life, or what we considered the most important parts of growing up. Then she would sit back and listen carefully to our free-flowing discussion. From time to time she would go into the house and come back with a book or *New Yorker* magazine. "If that's what you think," she'd say, "then you should read this. I'd like to know what you think of it." Sometimes the reading agreed with one's point of view and added a new dimension; other times it presented a different point of view and made one think a little harder. She would chastise us only if we spoke without thinking through our point. "Don't you think it would help if you took just a minute to compose your thoughts before going off half-cocked, Frances?"

As we grew older, the teas were replaced with less formal visits. The same sorts of subjects were explored, magazines and books dispensed, and mild criticism leveled if we had neglected the books that Grams thought "surely by now" we would have read.

OVER THE YEARS, I tried to make sense of my world. From the people who were close to me, I received a framework of assumptions, rules, and beliefs into which I tried to fit all the new pieces of information that came my way. It was a little like solving a jigsaw puzzle. Inevitably, a few pieces came along that didn't quite fit with the worldview I'd been given or that seemed to belong to another puzzle entirely.

All of my elementary school classmates were middle-class kids from town. When we went on to the larger junior high school, we were kept in the same homeroom class. I might have grown up believing that everyone in the world was just like me if I hadn't decided to take band. That change resulted in my moving into a different homeroom—the homeroom of leftover kids. This class included a girl with cerebral palsy, a mentally-retarded girl, and children from poor farm families. Unlike the kids in the more homogeneous classes, no one in this homeroom cared if you had a Jantzen sweater.

My new homeroom was much more alive. There was more texture in the environment; it made school less boring. That's where I first noticed the joy of diversity.

I was a Camp Fire Girl, and when I was about twelve, one of our group projects was to sew and embroider a needlework layette—a set of blankets, clothes, diapers, and booties for a newborn baby. When it was finished, we took our layette to a Mexican farmworker family that was expecting a baby. The family picked potatoes on the large ranches and farms owned by my parents' friends. When I saw how the Mexicans were cramped together in that farm labor camp, eight people to a room, I was stunned. The wonderful Christian people I knew—how could they let their workers live like this? It just didn't make sense to me that the same ranch owners who were so nice to me could live so well while the people they employed lived so badly. I went home and cried all night. The Johnsons and the Hennys, the upstanding people in our community, who were in our church!

Around the same time, I was very much moved by a speech I read. It was by Chief Joseph of the Nez Perce Indians of northern Idaho. An eloquent pacifist, Chief Joseph had tried to avoid war with white settlers. But some of the young men of the Nez Perce had gone against his wishes and had responded to the settlers' provocations. The ensuing battles resulted in many casualties for the Nez Perce. Then, as the Indians tried to retreat to Canada, General Oliver O. Howard's troops cut them off and decimated them. The speech I read was the one Chief Joseph delivered when he surrendered in October 1877:

> Tell General Howard I know his heart. . . . I am tired of fighting. Our chiefs are killed. Looking Glass is dead. The old men are all killed. It is the young men who say yes or no. He who led the young men is dead. It is cold and we have no blankets. The little children are freezing to death. My people, some of them, have run away to the hills and have no blankets, no food; no one knows where they are, perhaps freezing to death. I want time to look for my children

and see how many of them I can find. Maybe I shall find them among the dead. Hear me, my chiefs, I am tired; my heart is sick and sad. From where the sun now stands, I will fight no more forever.

I had already been exposed to pacifist ideas by my grandmother Peavey. She would often say that all wars are economic wars, and that "peace at any price" should be our goal. Grams was proud that none of her relatives had fought in any wars.

And yet Grams and Grandpa had been friends of General Howard! Members of my family had been part of the community that supported his efforts to conquer the Nez Perce. General Howard had even given my grandmother his family's christening dress. All the Peaveys had been christened in it, and it was part of the legacy I was to inherit. We had a direct relationship to the fact that the Nez Perce had been slaughtered and had lost most of their territory and sovereignty.

The first time it occurred to me that our government might do something wrong was in the early 1950s, when Julius and Ethel Rosenberg were convicted of conspiracy to commit espionage, and then executed. I read in *Time* magazine about people protesting the Rosenbergs' death sentences. And I took out the magnifying glass to examine the demonstrators' faces. I had never before heard of people protesting, but somehow I identified with them. I understood that we make mistakes in this country but we try to fix them.

My dad used to take one or another of us kids on trips to learn about farming. It was always a lot of fun. We'd drive to the different farms he supervised in the towns near Twin Falls. The farm women would sometimes serve us pie or give us chickens to take home.

Our route would often take us to Paul, Idaho. As we drove through, I remember my dad getting a hurt look in his eyes. A terrible thing had happened here, he would tell me. During World War II, Japanese-American citizens had been put in a relocation camp in Paul. "You always have to try to keep these things from happening," my dad told me. "Our government has done it once, governments have done it in the past. It's very, very wrong." He told stories of his family's visiting the Japanese families interned at Paul and taking blankets to them.

BY THE TIME I WAS IN HIGH SCHOOL, my greatest goal was to leave Idaho and go to Macalester College in St. Paul, Minnesota. My father had already decided that all of his children would go to Idaho colleges, marry Idaho spouses, and stay in Idaho, so he could play with his grandchildren. (Besides, he couldn't imagine that anyone would ever want to live anywhere besides Idaho.) So at Christmastime of my senior year in high school, I said I didn't want any presents; I only wanted permission to go to Macalester College. My parents said no, and gave me presents. I remember getting an Omega wristwatch. I was miserable.

I started at the College of Idaho in 1959 but two years later managed to transfer to San Francisco State College.

In the fall of 1961, SF State was alive with political excitement. A year and a half earlier, the House Un-American Activities Committee had come to San Francisco to hold hearings about Communists in California. Thousands of people had protested against HUAC at City Hall; some had been hurt, others jailed. When I arrived at SF State, there was still talk, inside and outside of classes, about that demonstration and about the battle to abolish HUAC.

There was another hot issue that year: the famous socialist Norman Thomas had been invited by the students to speak, and then the invitation had been mysteriously withdrawn. Students were furious and held a demonstration.

To get from one class to another, I had to walk past the "free speech area." Around midday, people would be holding forth, espousing their causes: socialism, communism, devil-worship, the Campus Crusade for Jesus. Whatever were the important issues of the day, people would get up and speak about them. It was impressive that people had the nerve to stand up and talk about such strange ideas. I thought the forum was great: in America, you stand up and speak. This was the First Amendment in action.

There were often announcements in the student paper about political, religious, or educational meetings at a building called the Gallery. I used to drop in and stand around the perimeter, listening. I remember civil rights meetings attended by thirty or forty people, mostly men, some black and some white. I would watch as one person after another made a point that was obviously very important to him. People would shout and gesticulate and carry on. I was fascinated but had no idea what was going on. For me, it was like going to the zoo.

IN 1963, AFTER GRADUATING from San Francisco State, I began teaching science to eighth graders at Roosevelt Junior High School. Every morning, as required, I insisted that students pledge allegiance to the flag. Often there were black kids who wouldn't say the pledge, and I had a hard time understanding that.

It finally got through to me one morning. I came to my first class—eighth graders who had been grouped together as slow learners—and began taking the roll. One of the kids bolted up and said, "What do you think about what your people did to our people last night?" He was referring to the bombing of a church in Birmingham—four young black girls had been killed. I'd heard about it on TV the night before but it hadn't particularly grabbed me. I looked up and all the students were paying attention, which almost never happened in that class. It was a holy moment. I knew we couldn't go on as usual; we had to address the issue immediately. I came out from behind my lectern and started talking about it with the students. One of them said, "And we're *not* going to salute the flag today!" I began to see what the flag meant to them. It represented a country that had broken its promises to them. "With liberty and justice for all? No way, Miss Peavey."

That was also the year that the NAACP arranged my black lessons. In return I did occasional volunteer work there—collating mailings, addressing envelopes, going door-to-door to publicize a statewide fair housing ballot measure. Some of those I canvassed didn't want to talk about the issue. Some got mad at me and slammed the door. I remember pressing my views on a sympathetic white woman: "We just have to *make* white landlords and banks treat Negroes fairly." She wasn't sure it was possible to *make* anyone do anything.

As the civil rights movement grew, I wanted to become a part of it, to do something besides learning about the black community and trying to be a conscientious teacher. I had fantasies of going to Mississippi to work for civil rights, but that never happened.

When I heard that there was going to be a demonstration to

demand equal hiring for blacks at the Sheraton Palace Hotel in downtown San Francisco, I decided to go. We all met at a church, then drove to the Sheraton Palace, went inside and sat down in the lobby. I had no idea of what was supposed to happen, so I just did what everyone else did and tried not to be conspicuous.

We all sang songs and listened to speeches. Then the police came and ordered us to leave. When we refused, they arrested us and took us to jail. It was a real surprise; in my naiveté I hadn't considered the possibility of getting arrested. But there I was in a cell with six or seven black women. Some were from our sit-in; others were more regular inhabitants of the jail. There was great singing in that cell—I remember especially "Down by the Riverside." But I felt shy and bewildered. I kept worrying that the other teachers at school would find out I was in jail. One of my cellmates had just begun to instruct me in the art of picking pockets when we were released.

After the sit-in, I sporadically attended civil rights meetings and speeches—still as an observer, never saying anything. I did take some direction from the meetings, boycotting restaurants and writing letters to congressmen. Although I didn't know how all this would result in better conditions for black people, I was willing to cooperate.

THE DAY JOHN F. KENNEDY WAS SHOT, my teaching supervisor came and told me the news. At lunchtime, I rushed down to the teachers' lounge where everyone was glued to the television. Parents were calling the school, asking us to tell their children about it. I went up to my fifth-period science class and said, "I suppose you have heard that President Kennedy has been shot." Some of the students started crying. One shouted, "It's the Republicans who did it!" Some of the black students were really scared and asked, "Does this mean we have to go back to slavery?" I realized how President Kennedy had come to personify their hope for equality.

I had admired Kennedy's gusto, straightforwardness, and quest to make things better, but I had never idolized him. For me the shock was that a president had been killed. I had associated assassinations with the unstable countries in South America that were having coups and insurrections all the time. Assassinations weren't supposed to happen in our country.

The shock was even greater when I heard the allegations that the CIA had colluded in the killing. Even the possibility that a part of our government could be involved in the assassination of a president had a powerful, disillusioning effect on me.

The assassinations of Martin Luther King, Jr. and Robert Kennedy in 1968 were further assaults on my belief that our democracy had civilized us.

I FIRST HEARD OBJECTIONS to U.S. involvement in Vietnam in the summer of 1966 while waiting in an office at SF State. A fellow graduate student started telling me that we had to get our troops out of Vietnam. My response was to defend the United States: there must be some good reason for our government to be involved over there; maybe we don't know all the facts. She told me that the Gulf of Tonkin incident was a sham, that U.S. ships had provoked the "attack" that was serving as the pretext for American military involvement in Vietnam.

As she talked, I began to waver in my opinion. Only a year earlier we had sent troops into the Dominican Republic—an action that I had considered wrong. Maybe our involvement in Vietnam was similar. The conversation, which must have lasted about an hour, ended with her inviting me to a meeting to find out more. I went, joining about a hundred people in a high school auditorium. That meeting raised more disturbing questions. Within six months I decided that we had no business being in Vietnam.

The Vietnam War convinced me that our government was doing something wrong. On the civil rights issue, I had retained some hope that the government was, in some instances, trying to act in the interest of justice. But how did our involvement in another country's civil war serve justice? And the war was costing us a lot of lives. For what? Nobody I knew was benefiting from that war: not my family, not the farmers in Idaho, not my college classmates. It appeared that the only needs the war served were internal to the government.

About the same time it started coming to light that the food we were eating contained dangerous additives and chemical residues. I would ask people, "Why would Kellogg's allow poison in the cereal? If they did, we would die and we wouldn't be able to buy cornflakes." For a long time I refused to believe the quacks who said BHA and sodium nitrate and DDT were bad for us. When someone finally convinced me that our food could be dangerous, all kinds of other beliefs crumbled. The food issue was a major step in the breakdown of corporate credibility. Things were not logical. Big businesses weren't thinking about my needs, about my body's long-term survival. And I had trusted them to do that! Like the government, they seemed to be serving only their internal needs—in this case, maximizing their short-term profit.

These discoveries were overwhelming to me and to many other people my age. If we couldn't trust our government or the food suppliers, we would have to take care of ourselves. To do that, we would need enormous quantities of information. Suddenly there was a quantum leap in the number of things we needed to be concerned about.

Just about the time we were getting ready to be responsible adults, the definition of responsibility changed. It was no longer enough to make a living, pay the bills, and prevent forest fires. Now we had to read the ingredients on every food package and comprehend the intricacies of foreign policy. And voting was no longer an adequate way of participating in the political process. Politics now seemed to require working all the time, informing ourselves and others, and pressing for change.

During the Vietnam War, I explored a wide range of political activities. I went to marches, worked on committees, and wore an armband during the invasion of Cambodia. I gave emotional support to a man I loved who was about to be drafted and was trying to get conscientious objector status. And I worked with a group in Los Angeles on an underground railroad for soldiers who had deserted the military.

Just hearing about the war on the news every night kept me feeling angry, crazy, and sad a lot of the time. One night I heard a story on a talk show about three U.S. soldiers in Vietnam. As one of the soldiers walked away from two buddies, he saw a Vietnamese girl run up, take a candy bar from them, and eat it. Then the girl reached inside her dress and there was a big explosion—the two soldiers and the girl were blown up. Her parents must have given her a hand grenade and sent her out to do this.

After hearing the story, I lay in bed and cried. What must it have been like for the Vietnamese family? I pictured them teaching the girl how to set off the grenade. How much desire to defeat the Americans lay behind the willingness to sacrifice their child? And the U.S. soldiers—what was it doing to them to know that they couldn't even share a candy bar with a child without fearing for their lives?

IN THE LATE SIXTIES and early seventies I saw a society shift. Even some of the most vociferous supporters of the war changed their opinions. Over and over I heard parents say, "My kids finally convinced me that the war was wrong." Friends would tell stories about encounters with their parents when they went home for visits. At first the parents would be angry about their long hair and their radical ideas. But often, if the kids kept the dialogue going, the parents would begin to listen.

Getting the United States disengaged from the Vietnam War was a slow process. In the early stages, anti-war sentiment was monopolized by ferociously determined young people. A subculture developed—we could tell who was "us" and who wasn't, based on length of hair and style of clothing. The movement was a tremendous force in our lives; we defined ourselves in relation to it.

Gradually the concern spread. For many people the turning point was in 1970, when National Guardsmen killed four student protesters at Kent State University. Eventually the battle against the Vietnam War was being fought on every front in the country: in board meetings, classrooms and workplaces, in courtrooms and Congressional hearings, at dinner tables and cocktail parties. That's what it took to shift the ground from which our Vietnam policy grew. And this shift set changes in motion elsewhere: old assumptions about education, authority, and family were all being challenged.

Having seen the movement against the Vietnam War from almost the beginning through to the end, I find it is a cornerstone in my understanding of how social change occurs. It gives me confidence that citizens can make a difference, not just in reforming existing institutions and processes but in making more substantive changes as well.

Although I am still proud of the work we did to end the war, a lot of what I learned from it was how *not* to make change. Seeing the news on television every night filled our lives with pain. We couldn't bear to have our country doing those terrible things in Vietnam. We were desperate to stop the madness, and as a result our work was often poorly planned. We had a lot of rhetoric but little coherent theory. We hadn't seen enough history to have much confidence in what we were doing.

We often treated each other with the same desperation we felt about the war itself. Meetings were filled with confrontation and accusation. Shouting matches and fistfights broke out as we tried to agree on "principles of unity" for a rally.

Black students were coming into their power, so there were a lot of struggles about racism among us. People were thrown out of meetings for being racist. We weren't very much aware of the issues between men and women, so the men controlled the decision-making and did most of the talking.

I remember going home from anti-war meetings thinking, "This is hopeless." But I kept going because of my anger about the war. I had to do something about it, and those meetings seemed to be "the only game in town."

IN THE YEARS since the end of the Vietnam war, social change has become my life's work. I have worked with Asian elders to prevent their eviction from a residential hotel, built a park with the down-and-out people of Sixth Street in San Francisco, helped launch a campaign in India to save the Ganges River, and performed comedy that illuminates some of the more absurd aspects of life in the nuclear age. Once a shy college girl who silently watched early civil rights meetings, I am now hired as a consultant to plan change.

This may appear to be a vast and impressive journey. But it has been comprised of many small, often barely perceptible choices. And each step has seemed to follow naturally from the previous one.

I have never lost my love for the United States. Even during the Vietnam War, when patriotism was unpopular, I still sang patriotic songs when I drove over the foothills and saw the Magic Valley of Idaho stretched out before me. Flag-burning at demonstrations always bothered me. I didn't want to burn the flag; I wanted to cleanse it.

I have always felt that my work for social change was patriotic. I want my country to be a better place, to be more responsive to the needs of the whole world. I have come to see that love for my city, my country, and my world need not be mutually exclusive. I've begun to feel patriotic about this planet.

3 | Connection in Action: The International Hotel

IF YOU GO TO THE INTERSECTION of Kearny and Jackson streets in San Francisco, you'll see an empty lot. That's where the International Hotel used to be, a place where thousands of people came to help elderly tenants in their struggle to save their home. I was one of those who came to help.

The International Hotel was an old four-story walkup in the heart of what used to be Manilatown. Rooms in the hotel averaged eight by ten feet. About a hundred tenants lived there, most of them older Filipino and Chinese people. Many had lived in the hotel for twenty or thirty years. They had built a community there.

Developers had been tearing down many of the older residential

25

hotels in the area in order to put up office buildings, hotels, and condominiums. It was unclear what the developers who bought the I-Hotel would do with the property, but it was clear that they wanted the tenants out.

The ten-year struggle for control of the hotel began in the mid-sixties. It was a complex drama involving many players: tenants, developers, lawyers and judges, a coalition of liberal and left-wing groups supporting the tenants, the mayor and county sheriff. I helped organize the tenants to resist eviction and plan strategy. During the last year before eviction, I lived at the hotel for weeks at a time.

Supporters contributed to the campaign in many ways. Each time eviction appeared imminent, thousands came to defend the hotel. As the empty lot demonstrates, the tenants were eventually evicted. In the end, nonviolent resistance was met with violence from the sheriff's men and the police. And the hotel was demolished.

But what happened at the International Hotel is much more than a landlord-tenant battle. For me it is a story of heart politics. At the I-Hotel I began to feel what it's like to work for change from the heart, and to understand how different that is from working for an abstract principle.

It was because of a principle, though, that I first went to the hotel. During a four-week trip to China in 1974, I had been deeply impressed by one of the guiding principles there: "Serve the people." The Chinese were building a society where from earliest childhood everyone was taught that the way to live a good life was to serve the people. So when the people at the I-Hotel put out a call for help, I went.

I joined the Internal Security Committee, which was in charge of supporting and organizing the tenants. Immediately I began not just to serve, but to develop a heart connection with many of the people there.

Wahat Tompao, a wonderful, kind man in his mid-seventies, had lived at the I-Hotel for many years. He was from a mountainous area in the Philippines. During World War II, he worked for the U.S. Army as a guide in the Central Pacific. Wahat had a tremendous dignity about him, as well as a great sense of humor. He loved to tease us. He would say, "I'm from the mountains, where people eat dog!" Then he would laugh at how repulsed we Americans would be.

Felix Ayson always felt he was close to death. A deaf man and a Marxist, he was always teaching the organizers around him, sharing books and wisdom, and sharply criticizing anyone whose actions were based on a narrow political analysis. Felix's room was full of books, and he had a cat who notified him when someone was at the door. He died a year after the eviction.

Mr. Yip was a spry Chinese alcoholic who walked in and out of meetings and was not very much involved in preventing eviction, but still did what he could.

Alfredo and Luisa Delacruz were a quarrelsome Filipino couple. Mr. Delacruz had been a seaman but couldn't work much anymore because of a mental disability. Mrs. Delacruz was one of the most powerful and respected tenants. No one at the hotel called her Luisa—she was "Mrs. Delacruz" or "Mama D." A strong and proud woman, she worked as a master fabric cutter in a shop that made jewelry display cases. In the Philippines she had participated in union drives at American-owned brassiere plants.

Emil DeGuzman was a young Filipino community organizer whose father had lived in the hotel. It was easy to love Emil, a humble yet strong-willed leader who was devoted to the residents of the hotel. His work and his understanding of strategy had drawn him further and further into the campaign until he was living at the hotel and working there full-time.

Felipe Daguro, a longshoreman, wore nickels inside his ears. On his payday he would press money into my hand to help with the struggle.

King San, a charming four-year-old, roamed Kearny Street in total safety. He was the son of a Chinese couple who ran a second-hand store on the ground floor of the hotel. King San spent most of his days bumming quarters from tenants so he could buy sodas.

As I got to know the tenants, I grew to love many of them and appreciate the community they had built. The I-Hotel was more than simply a shelter for its tenants. For decades it had been a cultural center for Filipino and Chinese people. It was a place where seamen lived between journeys. Filipino migrant workers stayed there after working summers at the crab and salmon canneries in Alaska, or picking grapes in California's Central Valley. The hotel was a place to get mail and to hear news from the Philippines. Emil remembered going to the hotel as a boy and seeing fifty or a hundred people standing outside talking. Tenants ate holiday dinners together and invited lots of neighbors; they shared their celebrations and their funerals.

The kitchen was one of the centers of the community. Most people who live in residential hotels have to eat restaurant meals (which are expensive) or cook in their rooms on hotplates (which are illegal). The I-Hotel was one of the last residential hotels in the city where people could cook. The kitchen, on the second floor, had an eight-burner stove and a sink. And somehow the seventy or eighty people who used it managed to avoid kitchen squabbles, which was incredible to me. If someone came in and all the burners were in use, he would simply come back later. Often people cooked for each other, especially for those who couldn't take care of themselves.

THE INTERNATIONAL HOTEL CAMPAIGN offered outsiders many chances to work directly with the tenants. Some supporters, like those of us on Internal Security, got to know the tenants by organizing a tenants' association, going door to door in the hotel sharing news and finding out what they thought should be done. We had brunches every Sunday to talk with the tenants about new developments and to hear their thoughts.

When eviction was threatened, hundreds of volunteers would sleep on the floor of the hotel, taking turns doing night watch duty and then going off to 9–to–5 jobs in the morning.

Doctors, nurses, and paramedics got to know the tenants through their work on the Medical Committee. Facing eviction is stressful, and some tenants worried about what the strain would do to their health. The medical people gave the tenants regular check-ups, kept records on their health, and taught them what to do if someone had a heart attack.

People from political and community groups supported the struggle by sitting security watches. We always had two people by the front door watching who went in and out of the hotel. Sabotage and arson were constant threats. A fire set in the I-Hotel three years before had killed three people; while I was living at the hotel, another hotel around the corner was torched. During the day tenants stood many of the watches; at night, community groups took over. One of the two nightwatch people had to walk through the hallways every hour, see that everyone was okay, and make sure the fire extinguishers were in place. The tenants knew that if they felt anxious in the middle of the night they could come down and talk to the security watch. This turned out to be an important organizing idea. On these four-hour security shifts supporters got to know and like the people they were fighting for; they began to fight for reasons beyond ideological ones.

Not all of the contact with the tenants was pleasant, of course. Every week someone from Internal Security had to take Mrs. Knowles to the supermarket. Mrs. Knowles was an elderly white tenant who wanted help with her grocery shopping. She had quite a few cats and liked to complain a lot. Taking Mrs. Knowles shopping really tried one's patience, but it had to be done. That was part of our political work.

Then there was a tenant who wasn't able to control his bowels. Every week someone from Internal Security had to go clean his room and wash his clothes. People would feel sick; I used to throw up after cleaning his room. At first I thought we should throw him out of the hotel, and even said so in meetings. But later I realized that we had to work out our relationships in a way that didn't exclude him, because he was in our world. We can't dispose of people just because they displease us or have a habit we don't like. He was an alcoholic and did the best he could. Cleaning him up was part of serving the people.

As I became more deeply involved at the I-Hotel, I got more opportunities to serve the people. One night, someone from the security watch called me out of a meeting to tell me that Mrs. Delacruz was threatening her husband with a knife. When I reached the manager's office, Mrs. Delacruz was sitting there staring at the TV and clutching a knife. Mr. Delacruz wasn't around. I sat down and watched television with her until she seemed more composed, then asked what was going on. She told me that her husband had insulted her and she was going to kill him. I asked her to give me the knife; then we would go find him and work this out. She refused, bolted for the door, and ran downstairs to the recreation room, where Mr. Delacruz had gone. I got in front of the door, and insisted that she either give me the knife or allow someone to go in with her, to keep her from hurting him. She threw several chairs at me. Tenants and supporters were peeking down the stairs, ready to help if I got in real trouble.

When Mrs. Delacruz finally got into the recreation room, I was with her, and Mr. Delacruz had a man with him. Conflict in Filipino society is frequently dealt with through intermediaries. I didn't know what to do, so I followed the lead of my Filipino counterpart. By the time Mrs. Delacruz and I left, she and her husband had reached a settlement: he agreed to sleep on the rec room sofa for a few nights, and she, in return, agreed not to kill him.

The next day, Mrs. Delacruz asked me to dinner to thank me. "I want you to call me Luisa," she said. "I like you. You don't let me become a criminal."

MEMBERS OF THE I-HOTEL community also connected with other people and their struggles. Some tenants joined the occupation of the Federal Building in San Francisco by a coalition of groups demanding access for disabled people. Some went to Sausalito to help save houseboat residents from the sheriffs and bulldozers. Urban poor people were fighting for hippies! I remember Wahat going up to an older man in the houseboat group and advising him about how to resist. "Use the old men," he said. "Old people are good to put on the front lines. Young people should hide behind us."

The tenants even felt connections with tenants portrayed in a movie. During the times when eviction seemed imminent at the hotel, we often showed the movie *Salt of the Earth*. In one scene the sheriff who has come to evict a family carries their belongings out the front door; the women carry them in again through the back door. The tenants loved this scene. They stood up and shouted, "Go! Go! That's what we're going to do!" They were animated for hours afterward. It meant a great deal to have a mental image of what eviction might be like and what we could do. Sometimes, responding to shouts of "Show it again!" we ran the movie twice a night.

As the I-Hotel struggle progressed, people with all sorts of talents came forward to help. Welders made special brackets to brace the doors. Telephone installers put in a telephone system and debugged it regularly. Someone from the squatters' movement in England showed us how to use bedsprings to barricade doors and keep the sheriffs out. The Food System, a network of cooperatively-run businesses, pledged hundreds of dollars' worth of food, so that if we were able to resist eviction for several days, people wouldn't go hungry. On particularly tense nights entertainers came in and lightened our spirits.

Whatever we needed, we put the message out through the phone tree, which was the alert network we set up to transmit information to supporters. When we were fortifying the hotel, an elderly Chinese tenant, Mr. Chung, was reminded of his experiences during the Russo-Japanese War. "We had to keep the Japanese from coming upstairs," he said, and he showed us how to barricade the stairs using plywood and two-by-fours. We put out our need for wood through the phone tree. And the wood came.

Thousands of people were on the phone tree, which was used to get materials, find people with special skills, and announce demonstrations. When we were threatened with eviction, supporters had to tell their contact people on the phone tree where they could be reached. On a trial run we were able to get over a thousand people to the hotel in an hour. Supporters gave the hotel a high priority. I often overheard people make plans with friends and then say, "I'll be there if they don't need me at the hotel."

Although resistance to eviction was our most visible strategy, a number of complementary efforts were going on simultaneously. Lawyers worked on eminent domain—a plan for the city to buy the hotel from the landlord and turn over management duties to the tenants. Others worked on a buyback plan—the hotel would be bought with federal monies, and the tenants would buy it back over the years through their rent. And there was a campaign to have the hotel declared a historical landmark.

On Saturdays we often planned strategy, discussing which forces were for us, which were against us, and how to turn the situation to our advantage. We identified various objectives and all the possible ways of attaining them. Then we focused on how to achieve our most immediate objective. By analyzing why different groups and individuals in the city had chosen to support us, we developed ideas of how to appeal to others less favorably disposed.

WORKING FROM THE HEART, I found, does not make politics clear or simple. The I-Hotel situation was complex, often confusing, and continually shifting. Our campaign was full of dissonance and internal problems. As we fought to save the hotel, I was often unsure what was the best course of action.

The deepest internal conflict centered on the manager of the hotel, Joe Diones, a Hawaiian-born Filipino and a well-known figure in the community. Joe was a short old man with a bulldog face, a former longshoreman who had been involved in labor organizing in Hawaii. Now he owned a nightclub in San Francisco. He had named himself manager of the hotel in 1969, when the tenants had begun to manage the hotel themselves.

Diones had been working against eviction, but he wanted to have all the authority himself. He didn't want a board of directors or a tenants' association that made decisions on a more democratic basis. He withheld financial records. And he threatened tenants and abused them. He kept a baseball bat in his office as a weapon, and he had two big "goons" who intimidated the tenants.

The Internal Security Committee decided the best way to stop eviction was to form a strong tenants' association. So I spent as much time in my first five months at the hotel fighting Joe Diones as I did fighting the developer or City Hall. Residents were slow to endorse a tenants' association—they disliked Diones but were afraid of him. We had to have our organizing brunches on Sundays, when Diones went to Reno to gamble.

Eventually we took a vote, which the tenants' association won. But then Joe Diones wanted to be president of it. He threatened to resign if he wasn't elected, while his goons walked menacingly around the meeting room. Diones was elected by a one–vote margin.

The tenants eventually threw Diones out of the hotel. It happened because one day he went too far. Very early that morning, sheriff's men had gotten past the security watches, entered the hotel, and posted eviction notices on all the doors. (Posting notices is a necessary legal step in the eviction process.) The tenants came out of their rooms to see what the commotion was about. They saw Joe Diones ranting and raving, blaming the watches, who were from the Food System.

But privately Diones told a tenant named Moonding, "I knew the sheriffs were coming." Now Joe may or may not actually have known; he may just have been trying to show Moonding he was in control. Moonding did some janitorial work for Joe and was somewhat dependent on him. But when he heard Joe say that, Moonding turned against him. He yelled to everyone, "Joe knew!" And when Joe went out for breakfast, Moonding grabbed some rope and tied the front door closed. When Diones returned, the tenants refused to let him in.

After he had been kicked out, Diones went to many liberal leaders in the city who had supported the I-Hotel tenants. He told them that young radicals and communists had taken over, that no old people were left in the hotel. This wasn't true, of course. All but one or two tenants stayed right through eviction. But city leaders tended to accept Diones' story. They were increasingly coming under attack for their support of the tenants, and Diones gave them an "out." The news media, too, tended to believe Diones' story.

Another source of internal conflict was the continual bickering among political groups. The key groups in the I-Hotel coalition were the I Wor Kuen (a Maoist group), the Katipunan ang mga Demokratikan Pilipino (Filipino Marxists), the Revolutionary Communist Party, and the anarchist-oriented Food System. Half a dozen community and religious groups also participated in the coalition—including the Human Rights Division of the Catholic Archdiocese, the American Friends Service Committee, and People's Temple. Mini-coalitions formed, with the Food System usually working with IWK, KDP moving back and forth, and the other groups on the sidelines trying to figure things out.

Arguments focused on how to define the I-Hotel campaign. Each of the sectarian leftist parties had a different "line," based on its own political analysis of the situation. IWK's line was, "This is a Third World struggle." KDP said, "This is a housing struggle." RCP had another line. The groups fiercely debated what our chant should be: "Third World communities unite!" or "Everybody needs a home!" We managed to resolve the issue by giving equal time to the different chants.

The competitiveness baffled me. Weren't we fighting for Third World people *and* for housing? Each group's Marxist dialectics had led it to its own "correct" analysis, and analysis affects strategy. The IWK tried to convince everyone else to concentrate on organizing support for the hotel in Third World communities. The KDP wanted everyone to organize among other tenants' groups. Neither group could entertain the possibility that two different analyses can be true at the same time.

My position was that we should proceed on every level, and that if anyone should be in control, it was the tenants: the people who have the most invested should have the greatest say.

Which brings me to my greatest internal conflict. Early on, I had been given the job of developing the tenants' plan to resist eviction. If the sheriffs, the police, or the National Guard came to evict the tenants, what would we do? I guess nobody else wanted to think about that. But having grown up with an insurance man for a father, I've always been preparedness-oriented.

I went at the job with gusto. We formed a Tenants Eviction-Resistance Committee and polled people about strategy. I worked with the tenants on an alert system and barricades. But the first time eviction seemed imminent, I realized that too much power was in my hands. Every decision was checked with me. I couldn't even go to the bathroom without someone running up with a question. I, who advocated that the tenants should be in charge of their own struggle, was in the position of controlling everything!

I don't know when I've ever felt so tired, so alone, and so despairing. During the first eviction scare, I lived in fear for three days straight: working with little sleep, solving problem after problem, I lost perspective on the situation and became totally drained.

This experience taught me that it's not enough to translate a heart connection into commitment and hard work. You have to translate it into *appropriate* work. The situation called for me to share power, to trust people more, for my sake as well as the campaign's.

A court order delaying eviction gave me time to figure out how to delegate much of my authority. By the second eviction period, we had floor captains and area captains, all tenants. And we were able to consult among ourselves from our different stations in the building, using the internal phone system.

FINALLY, IN AUGUST 1977, all the legal and political obstacles to eviction were gone. On August 4, the indicators started coming in; eviction was about to happen. We had scouts watching all the police stations, people roving the city with CB radios, informants in the jail, city bus drivers ready to report on the movements of police. Now all of them started calling in. Internal and External Security went on red alert and put the message out over the phone tree. Supporters started pouring down. In meetings, concerts, and movie theaters, announcements were made that the I-Hotel was on red alert, and large numbers of people stood up and rushed to the hotel.

Supporters knew that they could get up-to-date information by listening to KPFA, a local progressive radio station. KPFA started broadcasting from the fourth floor of the hotel at seven o'clock that night. We would give the announcer messages: "We've just had a call that the Washington Street freeway off-ramp is closed. Please re-route and come to the hotel immediately. You may park at such-and-such a place."

In the evening we had had a "tenants only" meeting. It was very quiet, a little like a funeral. The Tenants Eviction-Resistance Committee announced that eviction seemed to be about to happen. A tenant captain handed out a prepared sheet explaining what tenants should do with their valuables. There were a million questions in everyone's mind. Some people cried; everyone was filled with fear. What would eviction be like? What would we do if police entered the building? Would people be hurt? We knew we were in for a long night. Mr. Chung got drunk early.

By 10:00 P.M., three or four thousand people were waiting in front of the hotel with their arms locked together and hands clasped. Another four hundred were inside. From the hotel we watched the first police arrive, in full riot gear. Suddenly, a contingent of a hundred supporters on our front lines just walked away. The rest of the supporters were confused: why had that group pulled out? They had no way of knowing that the people who left were all from the Revolutionary Communist Party. The RCP apparently had a plan, kept secret from the rest of the coalition, to walk away when the police arrived. People from the IWK, the KDP, the Food System, and nonaligned supporters held their ground.

Bus drivers called in to report that police were heading toward the hotel on horseback. At one strategy meeting we'd considered spreading marbles—which horses can't walk on—but the idea was never followed up. We didn't think they would really bring horses to break through a nonviolent line. But soon we could see the mounted police approaching.

As we watched what was happening in front of the hotel, we heard a commotion on the roof. The roof strategy had always been our weakest. We knew we couldn't depend on the assurances we had gotten: from the Police Department that they wouldn't try to enter the hotel from the roof, and from the Fire Department that they wouldn't allow their equipment to be used for a roof landing. We had identified the roof as a site of potential violence: it was not visible to supporters or observers on the street below. So we had put our most reliably nonviolent people up there—people from the Archdiocese and the American Friends Service Committee.

Looking through a window and up the catwalk, I saw police on the roof in riot gear, carrying rifles. They had used a Fire Department hook-and-ladder to land. We had constructed poles with hooks to keep the hydraulic fire ladders from landing, but our poles had not held.

The four hundred police officers in front of the hotel had no idea how hard it would be to get through our lines of supporters. Even with their nightsticks, they couldn't get through. The locked-arms strategy was effective. Finally the police had their horses rear up and come down on people. Blood began to flow.

Throughout the struggle the tenants had said that the most important thing in fighting eviction was that no one should be hurt, that no harm come to their supporters. They had clearly said, "If people start getting hurt, we want to call off the blockade." Wahat had taken an especially firm stand on this issue. But now, when External Security captains asked supporters to move, they refused. The earlier unexplained departure of a hundred fellow supporters had caused them to lose faith in the leadership. "We came here to fight for the tenants and we're not leaving."

I saw Wahat standing at the window. His face was ashen. He said, "Call it off. Tell them to move, we'll leave. We don't want anyone hurt." A little later someone found him in his room, trying to hang himself. Floor captains moved all the tenants to the first and second floors so no one was alone.

Outside, the police violence continued. Our supporters were entirely nonviolent. Even if you want to fight, you can't when your arms are linked to the people on both sides. By the next day, about seventy-five of our people had reported to the hospital with injuries.

It took the police three or four hours to get through the crowd. At two o'clock in the morning the sheriffs came in to evict. The calmest, jolliest guy was the first sheriff to come in. Looking at his face, I knew he was a good person. But I also knew he was doing something that wasn't right. I had never thought much about chants, but a chant came to me that moment: "Where are you going to live when you get old?" As we took up the chant, I realized that's what we white people had been fighting about. That was our issue; deep inside of us we were fighting for old people.

They broke my tailbone. Emil and I were the only two people on Internal Security who were injured. We were also the only Internal people whose pictures had been in the newspaper. I was dragged by my feet, boom boom boom, down the stairs, and every time I landed on my tailbone I knew it wasn't helping any.

AFTER WE HAD BEEN REMOVED from the hotel, we were led outside the police cordon a block away. Standing there, looking at the hotel, was one of the saddest and loneliest moments of my life. We had given it our best, and had lost.

We waited there, greeting the tenants and supporters as they came out, hearing each of their stories, learning the latest details of what was going on inside the hotel. The supporters from the roof were the last to come out. They showed us their bruises and told a horrible tale. Out of the view of the news media, police officers had run amok, beating up the thirty unarmed and nonviolent members of our roof team, being especially brutal to anyone who wasn't white. I began to wish we had left the roof undefended.

My tailbone hurt so much that I couldn't sit, so I lay down on the sidewalk from time to time. We were all exhausted; most of us hadn't slept for twenty-four hours. Then it struck us—our denial that eviction would really happen had kept us from making plans for what to do afterward. The city had arranged for hotel rooms scattered all over the city, still failing to recognize that this was a community, that the tenants needed to be together, especially during this difficult and disorienting period.

Someone had the idea of parading through Chinatown and holding a press conference in St. Mary's Park. So we did that. I stood on the edge of the crowd. It was 6:00 A.M. by now, and there were only a few hundred of us left. We were a ragtag group. I looked at the faces of the tenants, thinking of how I felt about them, what I knew they had been through, and what their lives would be like now. Wahat spoke, dignified as ever, defiant and proud. I remember him standing on a ledge, his hair blowing in the breeze. He said, "I don't know where we are going or what is going to happen to us. We are grateful to all of you who stood by us and helped us. There are many people who don't understand why the hotel is important to us, but we know and we will always know." Some people cried. I didn't. I was too tired to cry, too shocked at being out on the street instead of inside the hotel with my friends.

An as-yet unopened drug rehabilitation center in another neighborhood offered its quarters to the tenants, and they went there in supporters' cars. They lived there together for a few days and then dispersed, a number of them moving into the Stanford Hotel on Kearny Street, three or four blocks from the I-Hotel.

Our last hope was that through court action the hotel would be given back to the tenants. Soon that hope was gone too. Several months after eviction, a man hired by the developer rammed a bulldozer into the hotel, leaving a gaping hole. This action was illegal. The developer didn't have a valid demolition permit, and by now the hotel was listed on the National Register of Historic Places, which provided temporary protection.

IN THE PERIOD OF HEALING and re-evaluation after the eviction I even questioned nonviolence. I began to see how terrorists are bred— by the frustration at the defeat of legal and nonviolent work. But the tenants I discussed this with straightened me out. How could they possibly live in a place that had cost someone's life?

Even toward the end of the struggle some people had believed that eviction might not happen. I had always thought it would. To me, the most important things were that it be done well, that people not be hurt, and that it be a lesson in what it means to take a stand with poor people. If we have that mental image, then we can do it again and again. For the most part it worked. Hundreds of white people grew closer to Filipino and Chinese people. After long years of isolation from one another, we had begun to make connections.

But people had gotten hurt. We had been lied to by the Police Department and the Fire Department. We had been betrayed by the Revolutionary Communist Party. The mayor, who had once promised he would not permit eviction, was on vacation in Hawaii when it took place. The sheriff, who had previously gone to jail rather than evict us, ended up presiding over the eviction. And we had lost the hotel. The tenants had been displaced. A community had been shattered.

Postscript

For seven years after eviction, the I-Hotel site remained vacant, its future uncertain. Just as this book was being completed, an agreement was reached among the developers, the city, and a community group. The developer is to construct two buildings on the block where the I-Hotel once stood, which will include 140 units of low-cost housing. Priority for occupancy will be given to former I-Hotel tenants, although how many of them will still be alive, reachable, or willing to move when the buildings are completed is anyone's guess.

4 | *A Sense of Place:*
Sixth Street Park

EVERY COMMUNITY has its untouchables. The rest of us tend to look away when we see them, trying to convince ourselves that their lives have nothing to do with ours. But this sense of separateness is an illusion. Untouchables are part of our world, and we are part of theirs.

Among the untouchables in the United States are the poor people and alcoholics who live on the street. In San Francisco, many such people congregate on Sixth Street, an area of rundown residential hotels, small liquor stores, and pawn shops. I worked with a progressive church to build and organize a park for the street people there.

In three years of working at the park, I tested many of my

assumptions about social change. I grew close to people at the bottom
of our society whom I never expected to know. Most of what I
learned has to do with the relationship of a society to its untouchables.
Issues of race, class, and violence figure prominently in this relationship.

Like the International Hotel, Sixth Street Park is now no more
than a vacant lot. Because it was a reminder of a painful situation,
the park became a scapegoat. Eventually real estate interests, politicians,
and journalists attacked it; the church retreated from its commitment;
the park was bulldozed.

The painful relationship between the untouchables and the rest
of society continues. Whether or not we acknowledge it, whether
or not we try to improve it, it is there.

WHEN I USED TO DRIVE along Sixth Street, I would see residential
hotels, men standing around talking, a lot of litter. But I didn't
spend much time thinking about the situation there.

In 1978 my friend Michael Phillips approached me about the
idea of buying a small vacant lot on Sixth and Minna Streets and
turning it into a park for street people there. Michael was working
as business manager for Glide Church, which was backing the project.
The vision that emerged was a park that would honor street people
and their problems. It would be a place for people who had no
place. No pressure would be exerted on people to stop drinking; in
fact, since the land was privately owned, people could drink there
without being hassled by the police. (Laws against drinking on the
street in effect discriminate against those who have no home to drink
in and who cannot afford to drink in bars.)

In thinking about plans for the park, I had to tune in to the
situation on Sixth Street. In my black lessons I had learned a little
about the street life of unemployed black men. In poor, urban black
culture, the street is a newspaper, a soap opera (for personalized
drama in life), a bar (where the cheapest wine is shared), a place of
business (where drugs, women, and stolen goods are sold, and where
contractors can find cheap labor), and a bank (where money is lent
or stolen). The street is also a therapist's couch, where people help
solve each other's problems, recounting troubling information over
and over until they make sense of it.

I remember going down to Sixth and Minna for the first time
with Gene Reed and Alvin Wise, two black men we'd hired to help

plan the park. A small crowd of street people was gathered around us. Out of nowhere a big man came up to me, took my arm, and said, "Come on baby, let's go." Bewildered, I told him I wasn't going anywhere. "But I already paid for you," the man said. "I paid that guy, and he said you'd come up to my room with me." All this time he was fondling my bottom. I realized what was going on, and told the would-be john that I was not for sale and that he should get his money back. He hurried down the block, shouting after "my pimp."

I felt afraid of the people on Sixth Street. Would they want my money? Would they hurt me? I found I was reluctant to love people who were in bad shape. And I felt guilty, because I suspected that I'd had more opportunities in my life than they'd had in theirs.

Gene and Alvin interviewed the street people to find out what they wanted in a park. And you know what they wanted? Garbage cans. Toilets. Grass. And showers. One of the first things we learned was that poor street people want to improve their lives. We commissioned three designs for the park, and Gene and Alvin took them back to the men on Sixth Street for comments. The final design reflected the lives of the park's users.

With the help of young people from the California Conservation Corps, we built a park on the 25-by-125-foot lot. It was the most compact park in the city, no bigger than the front yard of a modest suburban house. Walking into the park from the Minna Street alley, you'd see men gathered around a metal barrel with a fire burning inside. They'd be cooking stew on a grate atop the barrel, or just keeping warm. Next to the barrel was a small shelter with a corrugated metal roof and two walls—the kitchen area, complete with a picnic table and a nearby sink. The shelter also served to protect people from the wind and rain; often you'd see someone sleeping there. Beyond the shelter, steps led up to a small grassy knoll, which was far enough off the beaten path that the grass could survive. In the main area of the park, a few young trees and scrawny bushes clung to life.

Throughout the park, you'd see groups of men talking, eating, drinking. Some would be playing dominoes at one of the half dozen picnic tables; others would be sleeping on benches specifically designed to be wide enough to accommodate the weary. On the Minna Street perimeter were two chemical toilets, a tool shed, and an open dirt area with a basketball hoop—the court was used regularly. We defined the Sixth Street side with large jagged boulders, so park users would be less likely to sit there and harass passersby. In the center of the park was a water fountain, and nearby, set into the brick floor, we installed a bronze plaque honoring famous people who were alcoholics: Winston Churchill, Ernest Hemingway, W. C. Fields, Judy Garland, Ulysses S. Grant, Betty Ford, and so on.

Unfortunately, the logistics of installing a shower made it impossible. For a time we had "sleeping tubes" in the park—long corrugated-steel culvert pipes, four feet in diameter, with wooden platforms built inside. One year, during our annual park renovation, we installed a mural painted especially for the park. It depicted various aspects of life there: people sitting around the fire, staff meetings, a guy with a bottle staring off into the distance, people dancing and playing basketball.

DURING THE SIX WEEKS we spent constructing the park, I began to see how hard life was on Sixth Street. I worked there from 8:30 A.M. until 4:30 P.M., and every day at least one disaster occurred within two blocks of the park. A car crashed into the building next door, or a woman was run over, or someone was found dead. Police officers made arrests all the time.

Around me I saw men of all ages, sitting, standing, passing the bottle. In the early morning they were alert; their eyes caught everything that was going on. Some approached us to give advice and to offer help; others to flirt with women on the construction crew. But by afternoon, with a day's drinking and social interaction behind them, they were less coherent.

I continued to feel bad about the situation there. The dirt, the lice bothered me. And the lives that seemed to be passing without consequence. I kept wishing they could live more secure, fulfilling lives.

But I had to examine my discomfort in light of my culture and my values. Was it fair to assume that my kind of life was the one the men on Sixth Street would want to choose? Or that they would be able to choose it if they wanted to? Probably there were certain aspects of my life that they'd like to adopt, and others that would seem totally inappropriate to them. It wasn't for me to decide how they should live.

But to be able to work effectively on Sixth Street, I had to come to some understanding of why those people were there, doing what they were doing. Blaming either the street people or the society for their problems didn't help me. It only left me feeling bad about their situation, without having any ideas about what might improve it. I continued to ponder: Why are they there? How have any of us ended up where we are?

An early hypothesis was that the street people had chosen this way of life. But the more time I spent on Sixth Street, the more tentatively I held this hypothesis. I kept wondering: Could they have chosen otherwise, given the doors that had been closed on them by racism, poverty, and their consequent feelings of worthlessness?

ALTHOUGH WE DIDN'T WANT the park to be controlled by Glide's employees, we did have a few ideas we felt strongly about. We wanted the park to be kept clean, and we wanted a staff made up of people who used the park, who would take care of it and each other. As we got to know people on Sixth Street, we'd invite them to a staff meeting. Whenever someone would complain or make a suggestion, we'd say, "Come to the meeting."

An early concern in our meetings was that staff members were bullying people and collecting rent on the sleeping tubes. Another big issue was getting people to use the toilets instead of peeing on the flower beds. Park users were also pulling up flowers, leaning on fledgling trees, and using the tree stakes and parts of the underground sprinkler system as weapons. We worked on all these issues but before we could resolve them the potential weapons had been used up and the most vulnerable plants had died.

After about six months of staff meetings, we had a solid group. They were all alcoholics, and most of them were black. They had all served time in county jail, many in state or federal prison.

Askew was a bearded and greying man who walked with a cane. A grantwriter who had quit the 9-to-5 world, he talked slowly and ponderously—eloquently when he was at his best—and saw himself as a leader.

Godfather was a tall, slender man, a sometime-artist who always wore a cowboy hat and boots. Formerly a gardener, he began to care for the plants in the park.

Tony was a young guy from Louisiana who was, among other things, a mugger. During park construction he had been seen knocking over an old woman and taking her purse. Bird was a tiny fellow who looked like a sparrow. Because he was always threatening people, he'd been barred from all the institutions in the city that help poor people and alcoholics. Bird and Tony were buddies. A street drunk, I learned, almost always has a buddy, someone to watch out for him, to make sure he isn't attacked or robbed when he's asleep.

Hogshead never came to meetings but was sort of on the staff anyway. He was the wood gatherer. Hogshead was one of the ugliest people I've ever seen—his face was distorted, he was filthy, there was always slobber in his beard. Twice he vomited on me. It was an act of courage for me to shake his hand. Extending his dirty hand in friendship was a money-making scheme of Hogshead. When people would refuse to shake his hand, he could count on them to give him some "spare change" as guilt money. The park staff would often report, "Well, we cleaned up Hogshead today." That would be a victory. They would have taken him up to someone's hotel room, bathed him, and gotten him some clean clothes somewhere. Often they had to delouse him. That took a special kind of love.

Early on, the park staff trained me to respect their authority. My inclination was to walk into the park, say hello to everyone, meander. The park staff made it clear that when I arrived, I was to report to them first—to see how things were going and find out if there were any problems.

Glide Church never paid anyone to clean the park. The people who used it kept it clean, though sometimes it took some prompting if they had let things slide for a few days. Once in a while I'd come in and say, "Oh my, the park doesn't look so good today. Do you think you guys are going to—?" And they'd say, "Oh, we haven't started yet today! All our workers aren't here yet!" And if I picked up a shovel or a broom, somebody would just come and take it away from me. How would you feel if somebody came to your house and said, "Oh, I don't think your house is very clean, I'll just get to work and clean it"?

Different issues concerned the staff at different times. An early one was territoriality: some people had started pitching tents and others had been camping out in the sleeping tubes. We'd intended the tubes for transients, not full-time occupants, and so we decided to remove the tubes altogether. (There had also been public pressure against them: they were a disturbing monument to homelessness.)

But the biggest issue was always violence. How should it be dealt with in the park? A staff member would say, "I got hit on the side of the head when I was trying to break up a fight." Or a staff member himself had instigated violence: what should be done? So we'd re-enact the situation, with staff members taking the different roles. We also used role plays to explore other potentially violent situations. The staff concluded that when there was trouble they had to stick together: they *all* had to go to defuse the situation. For me it was wonderful to see some of the people who had perpetrated violence learning nonviolent techniques for resolving conflict. And the rate of violent crimes on that block actually went down during the tenure of the park.

BEFORE THE PARK EXISTED, people had congregated on Sixth Street without any collective purpose. Our job as organizers was not to define their purpose but to help it emerge. We tried to empower people without controlling them, to trust that they were more knowledgeable about their own lives than we were. We viewed ourselves not as the people with answers, solutions, or decisions but as facilitators, enthusiasts, support people. At the beginning I filled this role myself, but after a year I began to transfer much of the work to Karen Mercer. Karen's training included both social work and counseling, and I knew she would do a great job.

Traditional social change organizing assumes that the organizer is the resource—the person who makes things happen, solves problems, doles out the "goodies." At the park, the organizer's job was to help people look at their own resources. The organizer was a mirror, reflecting back to them what was presented and helping them figure out how to get things done that *they* wanted done.

Because the people felt it was their park, they took control and always made suggestions to improve it or to solve problems. When we were building the park, street people helped out with work and advice. "Listen, I used to mix cement for a living—let me show you how." During one of the spring refurbishings, the clay we put down on the basketball court got lumpy. We tried everything, but couldn't figure out how to fix it. A park newcomer came over and said, "I know a little about this. Could I have a rake?" He smoothed it out (and later joined the staff).

Staff members took their work more and more seriously, and after working together about three years they decided that members could not come to meetings drunk. (It had become apparent that disruptions and irrelevant digressions were instigated most often by members who were drunk.)

When people take on responsibility, they see themselves in a new way. A street person joins the staff of Sixth Street Park and becomes responsible for a corner of the world. He agrees to help keep the park clean, to take care of sick people, to break up fights. We helped this self-consciousness evolve by celebrating staff members' birthdays in the park (complete with cake), by giving out official staff jackets to members each year, and by issuing park staff I.D. cards.

There were also park membership cards for other park users. Staff members alone were authorized to hand these out and—if necessary— sign the member's card for him. The cards were a vehicle for bringing the park rules to everyone's attention. Those rules, set out by the staff and printed on the cards, were:

> No violence in park.
> No openly-visible weapons.
> All garbage in garbage cans.
> No gambling.
> No fires except in cooking area.
> No shooting up or sale of drugs.
> Curb your dog.

THE PARK PLAYED A VITAL ROLE in the city and the world: it was a point of connection with the down-and-out. It allowed outsiders to bring their resources to street people. I was amazed at the number of people who'd drive up and drop off a case of milk, or a bunch of sandwiches, or a load of wood for the fire. Karen remembers a young career woman, dressed in a suit and high heels, stopping by to drop off some homemade brownies in a box tied with a ribbon. Around Christmas one year there was a story on TV about the park. A few days later a big box of sleeping bags arrived from Los Angeles. Someone had seen the story, felt a connection with the people in the park, and made an appropriate contribution. That anonymous person's thoughtfulness made winter more bearable on Sixth Street.

Relations between street people and the police also improved somewhat. Captain Forni of the district police station came to a staff meeting and listened to complaints about a new beat cop who would go into the park, ask for winos' bottles, and pour their wine out on the street. Captain Forni agreed to explain to the cop that drinking was legal in the park. It was a friendly meeting—there was even talk of a softball game between cops and street people (which never happened), and I remember Bird asking Forni, "If I get arrested, can I call you and get out?"

At another meeting I asked the staff what they thought about nuclear power. Everyone spoke against it. So I invited them to a rally outside Pacific Gas & Electric headquarters in San Francisco, to protest the Diablo Canyon nuclear plant. We all had a wonderful time.

Sixth Street Park opened up exciting new possibilities in the relationship between a society and its untouchables. This excitement was picked up in early stories on the park in the *Los Angeles Times*, *New York Times*, *Wall Street Journal*, and on CBS-TV's Sunday morning show. People discovered that they had a desire to connect with street people, and the park made the beginnings of that connection possible.

But the park did not, as some might have wished, solve the problems of people on Sixth Street. It was no panacea. What was happening in the park was not so much solution as progress. The realities of life on the street stayed pretty much the same.

BECAUSE OF THE CONSTRUCTION of a huge convention center in San Francisco, many poor people have been forced to move from Third to Fourth Street and now to Sixth Street. They will probably continue to be moved as real estate values in the area climb. Many street people had grown up near the park—the neighborhood was their home turf. Others had come from out of town and made friends there. About half of those who frequented the park were on welfare or received some form of government assistance.

Many were shockingly young—in their twenties and thirties, though their faces looked much older. Quite a few park regulars were Vietnam veterans who had not been able to put their lives together after the war. For some men, there had been a major disappointment in family or work, and they had not landed on their feet.

Some lived in residential hotels, but many slept on the street. If you don't have a place to go, rain is a real problem. And cold. And where do you get clean? Where do you cook? Where do you have sex? These are the kinds of problems that people deal with when they have no place to live. And there are more and more people who live this way in our cities.

Why are people homeless? For one thing, there aren't very many vacant living spaces, and those that do exist are expensive. Even a small room in a residential hotel costs $200 to $250 a month. Street people don't have money for both housing and their addiction. Getting drugs or alcohol is a more pressing moment-to-moment need, allowing them to obliterate their sensitivity so that it's somehow tolerable to sleep outside. It's a self-perpetuating cycle.

Being poor is a full-time job. You spend your days traveling to the soup kitchen and waiting in line, often for hours. You spend your days trying to get welfare and food stamps—more long lines. If you don't have a birth certificate and an address, you can't get welfare. You are always looking for something that will keep you going for another week or another day—a safe place to sleep, a few dollars you can panhandle or steal.

If people at the park were representative, street people have particular difficulty holding on to money. Of course, they don't have much to begin with, but they seem unable to put their own needs above others'. If a street person has only a quarter and a friend comes up and says, "I need a quarter," he'll give it to him. Since they're in a situation where need is common, they're always broke. And yet they're sustained by each other. Multinational corporations make more by pooling their money. At the bottom it's exactly the reverse: street people pool their non-money, and all have less. And they steal from each other more often than they steal from outsiders. People become increasingly desperate toward the end of the month, as money from welfare and disability checks runs out.

Bea, one of several women who were park regulars, had continual problems with money. She is a gutsy middle-aged black woman who is strikingly good-looking when she's healthy. For awhile she kept her money in a metal box which she held under her arm. But when she'd fall asleep, someone would inevitably take the box. Then she put her money in her shoes, but they started taking off her shoes. There was really no safe place for her to keep any money.

But the despair isn't only economic. At its center is a hopelessness about life, which has become painful, degrading, out of control. Bea was always saying, "Things are getting worse"; that was almost a mantra for her. She was in the hospital on her birthday and was struggling with the question of whether she wanted to live. The doctor had told her she would be dead within a year if she didn't stop drinking. And she was about to go on trial for robbing a police decoy in the park. Getting sobered up looks good on your record. So she stopped drinking, then started again, and finally went into Detox. It is a familiar cycle.

The hospitals play a central role in the lives of street alcoholics. Many go into the hospital around Christmas, because they know they'll receive some attention there, be out of the rain and cold, and get fed decently. Sometimes the boost from a stay in the hospital can help an alcoholic change his life.

Street people experience much sharper ups and downs in their lives than I do. When they are up—a little chunk of money, a barbecue—they are really up. And when they are down—arrested, beaten up, very sick—they are really down.

And death is always close by. One day I heard that Godfather had left the hospital against the doctor's wishes and had come back to the park to die. I found him in a chair by the fire, slumped over, sleeping. The people sitting nearby explained that several weeks earlier Godfather had burned his leg at the fire. Gangrene had developed and Godfather had gone to General Hospital to have it looked at. They prepared to cut off his leg. Godfather was not in agreement about the amputation. They told him he would die if the leg wasn't amputated. It was at that point that he chose to return to the park to die whole among his friends.

Both the park staff and the church staff struggled with the question of responsibility. What should our position be? My own inclination was to try to talk him into going back to the hospital. But the park staff convinced me that we should respect his choice and help him live his last days in the park as he wanted to. I contacted the people at the neighborhood health center down the street from the park, and they agreed to visit Godfather once a day and to change his dressings.

Godfather stayed in the park all day and all night. Park regulars and staff covered him with blankets, coats, whatever they could find to keep him warm. They hustled up food from one of the free food places and cooked it for him on the open fire. And somehow, with all this intensive care, Godfather recovered. He retained his leg and he roamed the Sixth Street area for another three years, until he died in his sleep in a residential hotel room.

The staff had to have extra meetings to plan for Godfather's care. In one meeting they got to talking about how much they loved Godfather, and how they would miss him if he died, and several of them started to cry.

There are deaths on Sixth Street. There are shootings and stabbings, but more common are the deaths from cirrhosis and other ailments resulting from alcoholism and life on the street. When I got back from blockading Diablo Canyon in the fall of 1981, I found out that Hogshead had just died. We had a funeral for him at the park. Glide ordered a spray of flowers, and we put it in a raised part of the park. Street people made a semicircle of empty Thunderbird bottles and put a full bottle in the middle. In front was Hogshead's cup—because he always drank from a cup. People made short speeches. One said, "It's going to be colder around here, without Hogshead to get our firewood." And someone hoped that wherever Hogshead was, he was in a happier place than he'd been in on earth. For a long time after the funeral, when they passed the bottle, they'd pour a little in the flowers for Hogshead. Those flowers seemed to last forever.

Hogshead's official name was Clarence Thigpen and, years before, he had been a jazz pianist; I heard he played with Miles Davis's quartet. People used to say, "Hogshead would get his life together if only he could play." One day someone brought a piano to the park. Hogshead sat down at the piano, and he couldn't play anything. He started crying and said, "I'm too far gone. I'm never going to be able to play again."

I BASED MY WORK at the park on the assumption that people are more likely to allow the helpful, socially responsible part of themselves to emerge if they are treated with respect and confidence. But it will rarely emerge when people are under attack or in deprived situations. When people are downtrodden and everything around them is bleak, reflecting poverty and misfortune, the spark of hope inside an individual doesn't receive the fuel of outside confirmation.

Sixth Street Park nourished that spark of hope. It was designed to be a beautiful environment in a desolate neighborhood, a place where street people could work together for the common good. The park became its own subculture—an alternative context where a society's outcasts could articulate to each other their caring; could notice and appreciate their socially responsible behavior; and could call forth the best from each other. It was a context which increased the odds that people would act from their dignity rather than from the violent, desperate part of themselves. But it only increased the odds; it didn't eradicate violence and despair.

It was exciting to watch people at the park take on important work for the common good. Bubba was a big, tough bully when he came to Sixth Street Park. He joined the park staff after the staff had talked to him about not being violent in the park. And he began to use his size, his street smarts, and his hidden gentleness *for* people. He cooked for others in the park, started working on a place for park people to get mail, and became a self-appointed social worker for people looking for clothes, housing, or jobs. One night Bubba saw a man stabbing a woman in the parking lot next to the park. He started shouting in a pained voice, "Ooh! Ooh! That's too much stabbing—too much!" This broke the concentration of the stabber, who took off; his victim survived.

Mickey was a merchant marine whose commitment was to clean up fleas, lice, and venereal disease. He would take people to a hotel room near the park, put them in the bathtub, and clean them up. The local health center gave him a gallon of delousing shampoo. He also washed people's infested clothes. He was an alcoholic, in no better shape than the others, but he made a contribution to improving the world around him.

At one meeting I learned that the park staff had been taking care of a six-month-old baby. His father had brought him by and asked them to care for him. So someone at the park who was squatting in the nearby Pontiac Hotel cleaned up a room for the baby. The staff pooled their money to buy baby food, and they had developed a wild fantasy of raising the child themselves. So far they'd taken care of him for three days; the reason the issue got on the agenda was that they were worried the baby might be sick. Before we returned him to his father, I went down to the park and saw the baby, taking the sun. The two who took the most interest in him were Bird and Tony—the toughest, "baddest" guys in the park, the two I thought least likely to have a soft spot in their hearts. When a nearby drunk made some profane remark, one of them hissed: "Not in front of the baby!"

A particular event crystallized in my mind why this park was useful for the society at large. One day, outside the park but within view, a mugger tried to rob and beat up a woman. Someone in the park, one of the less regular visitors, saw the crime in progress and went out and broke it up. The mugger was not happy about this interruption of his economic activity. He went across the street to the liquor store and bought some toilet bowl cleaner. Then he returned to the park and threw it in the face of the man who had interrupted his crime. The lye burned the man's face, blinding him. The park staff called an ambulance, and he was taken to the hospital.

This event had been seen by several members of the park staff, and one of them, Tony, had gotten some acid on his sleeve as he tried to break it up. The culprit was arrested, and the district attorney wanted members of the staff to identify the acid-thrower at a hearing. This posed an ethical dilemma for the staff, especially Tony. Although he was very upset about the incident, coming forward as a witness for the state was another matter. Tony was a parole violator, and appearing in court could expose him to penalties— including more jail time. The staff discussion went on all morning; all the rights and wrongs were examined. Listening to it, I thought that this was one of the best and most unlikely places in the city for such a scrupulous ethical discussion. Tony finally decided to testify, and the group went along to support him (also to make sure he didn't chicken out, I suspect). Tony was very proud of his civic-mindedness and, as it turned out, they didn't check his record.

I WOULD LIKE to be able to tell you that Bubba, Mickey, Bird, Tony, and the other staff members never did another cruel thing, never mugged another passerby, never beat up another fellow street person—but this is not so. The park supported socially responsible behavior; but the situation on Sixth Street was still desperate. And much of the despair became manifest in violence.

Although violence is a part of all our lives, it's more apparent on Sixth Street, where the anger and hostility of black people at the bottom of society is always in the air.

I had a few direct brushes with violence at the park. The class differences between the park people and me were always evident, and they caused a lot of pain all around. Frequently people tried to hustle money from me; my standard response was "Do I *look* like the Bank of America?" But still they knew that I had money and they didn't; it was inescapable.

One day I was talking with a bunch of guys in the park who thought that I personally could help them out of their difficulties. I said: "You know, if I sold everything I have, and gave you all the money, things wouldn't be significantly better here." And I told them how much it pained me that things were so difficult for them.

When the discussion was over and I had started walking away, Bird stood up and said, "What if I pulled this gun out?" When he said that, his tone changed. Bird's hand was in his pants pocket, and I could see a small gun outlined there, its handle poking out.

"What would you do *then*?" I said forcefully.

He said, "Put it back in my pocket."

And I said, in my best schoolteacher voice, "Well, then just *leave* it there!" I turned my back and started walking casually to my car, all the time thinking: He's going to blow me away.

I got in my car, started it up, drove around the block and parked. And then I just shook and cried, I was so scared.

Another time someone pulled a shiv on me. A shiv is a piece of metal sharpened on both sides, and it was right at my neck—I could feel the cold metal. The guy holding it, someone I'd never seen at the park before, was saying in his toughest voice, "I could use this on you, or anybody, at any time."

And I—again the schoolteacher—said, "Oh, you should give that to me. We can't have knives in the park." Nothing happened for an instant, and then, taking the shiv away, I said, "I'll just put this in my pocket." And I did it. I stood there for a long time, just chatting, as if taking the shiv had been the most natural thing in the world.

I think that if I had acted afraid—either with Bird or with the shivman—I might have been killed. They were taking a certain posture ("I'm the baddest of the bad") and if you take the complementary posture ("I'm afraid of you"), then they may well kill you. You have confirmed the role they're playing. But if you take the position of being absolutely in control of the situation— that this is *not* to happen—then you kind of out-authority them. Sometimes this works.

This dynamic is at play all the time. When you're afraid, people sense it. Imagine how it makes them feel. If you walk into the park and I see that you're afraid of me, then who am I? Someone to be afraid of. You've confirmed my self-image; therefore, give me your wallet.

We must be very clear about this transaction. Each player in it is displaying only one aspect of himself. The postures we take toward each other do not only speak about us as individuals; they also express the interaction between us.

So before going to the park, I would always check to see whether I was disturbed, preoccupied, or distracted. In those states of mind I was more vulnerable, more likely to be a victim. Going to the park could also be more dangerous if I had unresolved difficulties with anyone. Once, early in the park's history, I had asked Tony to stop collecting rent on the sleeping tubes and to stop dealing drugs in the park. Our discussion degenerated into a screaming argument. Realizing later that losing my temper had been a mistake, and that violence was one of Tony's few options for retaliation, I decided to stay away from the park for about a week to let the situation cool off. And occasionally I intuitively sensed I shouldn't go to the park; I sensed danger. But when I had my wits about me, I almost always felt safe in the park. I came to trust that the staff would protect me: they wanted the park to survive, and violence would jeopardize that.

After Bird had threatened to pull the gun on me, I told Glide's minister, Cecil Williams, about the incident. The following day, Cecil dropped into a park staff meeting and took Bird outside for a few minutes. When the meeting was over Bird came up to me and said he wanted to talk with me. He took me around the corner, into a hallway, and I saw tears in his eyes. Bird said he was sorry that he had frightened me; he would never do that again. And he asked me to forgive him.

I think things had just gotten away from Bird that day. He had gotten overwhelmed and was grabbing at any straw to solve his problems. When he apologized, he said, "I didn't mean to hurt you." I know that's true. Even if Bird had blown me away—which I've always considered was possible—he wouldn't have meant to hurt me.

MANY OF THE PEOPLE AT THE PARK stopped drinking for short periods, but only a few sustained their sobriety. One successful quitter was Ben, a soft-spoken, physically strong man with tremendous integrity and leadership ability. He had been a professional clarinetist. Ben came to see me when his sister died. We talked for a long time, and he cried. The fact that his sister had died from an alcohol-related disease scared Ben enough to stop drinking.

Henry, Ben's buddy, was already on the wagon. A rotund, pleasant-faced man, Henry would sit in the park, silently watching everything that went on. Nothing escaped his vision; his presence pulled people to a higher standard of honesty. Henry came to be known as "Buddha."

Then Askew went into the hospital, and he decided to quit drinking, too. As he told it, "I thought about the park. I knew I had my work to do and I couldn't do it if I was drinking."

So Ben, Henry, and Askew stayed at the park, and their drinking friends agreed to support their abstinence. But sober, the three of them saw the park differently. Ben said, "I used to use alcohol to numb myself. Now that I'm not drinking, I see the pain of this place and it's killing me."

So we started an irregular group for people who were feeling the pain of the park. This "sensitives group" included Ben, Askew, Henry, Karen (the new park organizer), and me. We used the sensitives group sometimes to talk with other staff members if they were behaving badly at the park, and sometimes to provide personal help (Henry needed support to stop eating candy bars and ice cream). But mostly we talked with each other about how hard things were on Sixth Street. Ben, Henry, and Askew felt stuck. They were drawn to the park and to their friends, but it was cold and rainy there, and painful. Bea and Godfather were in especially bad shape. I began to understand how hard the change was for the three guys on the wagon. They had stepped outside of their old context, and seeing it from this new vantage point was excruciating. They wanted the situation to change for everyone at the park.

When you outgrow a situation, you sometimes have to divorce yourself from it to consolidate your gains. In the sensitives group, we discussed the idea of offering a clear conduit out of the park for those who needed it. But we decided that their leadership was important, both for themselves and for the park.

BY ITS VERY EXISTENCE, the park made the same pain that the "sensitives" felt accessible to the larger community. In July 1982 a reporter for the *San Francisco Examiner* wrote a long "exposé" attacking the park. I think the story was primarily an expression of the reporter's own anger and frustration with the plight of poor alcoholics and street people. The problems he described—violence, drug dealing, alcoholism, and illness—had existed on Sixth Street before, but the park made them more visible. It became easy for the *Examiner* and for politicians and city officials to blame the park, to make it a scapegoat.

The *Examiner*'s bitter reporting reflected the disillusionment the press often feels when a project, or a person, has flaws or doesn't *solve* a disturbing problem. We Americans tend to want quick solutions and have difficulty seeing things whole: the positive with the negative, the constructive with the destructive.

Perhaps we had been set up for the attack by all the glowing newspaper stories that had come out when the park opened. These stories had reflected journalists' desires to get connected with street people, with untouchables, and to know that their situation was finally being attended to. What a relief! Street people are real people, and this park is going to take care of them! We played along with the media hype, thinking positive publicity could only help the park. But it created unrealistic expectations.

Our failure to articulate clear and realistic goals for the park was a major mistake. We should have set as a goal a small reduction in crime in the area, rather than creating the impression that we would eliminate crime. We should have publicly acknowledged that alcoholics on Sixth Street would continue to die. And we should have used the early newspaper articles to demonstrate how difficult and often miserable life on the street is, rather than allowing a romantic "Aren't street people wonderful?" attitude to prevail.

Another major mistake was our failure to develop strong support for the park—including financial support—outside of Glide Church. Because it was under Glide's wing, the park was always dependent on the man at the top of the church hierarchy, minister Cecil Williams. And seeing life on Sixth Street was very painful for Cecil. In fact he rarely went to the park. When he did, he saw people like himself— black men—and they were in very bad shape. Cecil would often say, "We can't absolve our guilt by going down there." For a sensitive person like Cecil, the park must have brought up feelings of intense helplessness.

Cecil's political relationships in the city made the park even more vulnerable. In the fall of 1982, after the *Examiner* article had been published, the park came under increasing attack. The surrounding neighborhood was beginning to be "cleaned up" for the 1984 Democratic convention and a large office complex. When the park drew fire from Cecil's political allies, including Mayor Feinstein, he suddenly withdrew his support and made a unilateral decision to close the park. He offered jobs to Ben, Henry, and Askew. Other staff members were confused but offered no resistance. Some told me they felt betrayed.

I, too, felt deeply disappointed. But looking at all the factors involved, I concluded that the park couldn't be saved, that it was too late to organize it as an autonomous entity.

The park was fenced off and bulldozed, and the lot was put up for sale. The community ethic and sense of confidence which we had so carefully nurtured was destroyed. A place of beauty on Sixth Street was gone.

As I LOOK BACK on the work we did at Sixth Street Park, I think about the street people who at first seemed to me so different from people I knew. They are alcoholics in a society filled with alcoholics, many of whom work in the high-rise office buildings not far from Sixth Street. They are people prone to violence living in a violent society, a society that does violence to them daily. Yet they remain separate; they seem untouchable.

Sometimes I worried that in making my peace with the life on

Sixth Street I had settled for less than was possible. Askew, for instance, had left his wife, family, and 9-to-5 white collar job. Even though his present life didn't seem the kind I would want to live, I came to accept his choice. Someone else might come and save the people on Sixth Street. I was there to honor who they were and help them solve the problems *they* perceived in their lives, not the problems *I* had with their lives.

Friends would often ask me, "Isn't it hard to work at Sixth Street Park?" or "Isn't it painful to be around those people?" Certainly it was hard. Certainly it was painful. It was painful to see the illness, the addiction, the people out in the cold and rain. But what hurt me most was to hear people say that they felt useless.

The pain of working at Sixth Street Park was the pain of connection, the pain of loving people. Before I worked there, I had felt a different kind of pain—the pain of separateness, of being cut off from a whole group of my neighbors. That is perhaps more of a numbness than a pain. And now that I no longer work at the park, I feel a third kind of pain: the pain of a broken connection.

Since the demise of the park, most of the leaders among the staff have gone through rough times. Ben has been in and out of mental hospitals, with drug problems. Askew and Henry have taken up drinking again. I've lost touch with Bird, Tony, Bea, and the others.

I have heard about several parks designed on the model of Sixth Street Park: in Oakland, Los Angeles, Oklahoma.

But although there are increasing numbers of poor people in our country, their concerns are often disregarded. And I continue to wonder: How will we as a society learn to respect our untouchables? How will we create a context where they can respect themselves?

*What would I do with my last few minutes if the sirens went
off? Would I look out my window and watch it all go,
waiting that fraction of an eternity for the wave to evaporate
me? Would I grab whoever is nearby and give them all the
love I have? Or would I lie down on the hill near my house,
hug the earth like a dying lover, and apologize?*

5 | The Hidden Member
of Our Family

WHEN YOU BUILD a house yourself, it always feels a little more
fragile than other buildings you visit. You look at a wall and see
the individual two-by-fours and sheetrock. You know what's keeping
the windows from falling out, how the siding is nailed in place.
This is how I felt about the house I remodeled and lived in on
Potrero Hill in San Francisco.

One day in 1980, I was sitting in my living room reading the
newspaper. President Carter was threatening the Soviet Union with
nuclear weapons because the Soviets had invaded Afghanistan. I felt
cold and afraid. It started to sink into my consciousness that the
nuclear threat was serious and close, that our president was really
thinking about using those bombs. During the Cuban Missile Crisis
I'd felt certain that neither side would be stupid enough to use
nuclear weapons. During the Vietnam War some people worried
that the United States would use nuclear bombs. Not me. Even
while protesting against nuclear power in the late seventies, I didn't

61

give much thought to the other nuclear menace. But the way Carter was talking scared me.

Then it happened: the house rattled with a boom. It was a sharp jolt, and I knew that a nuclear bomb had exploded—over in Oakland, I guessed. In panic I dived to the floor below the window. As I cowered there, everything I had ever learned about nuclear bombs came into my mind. Don't look at the explosion or your eyes will melt and run down your cheeks. The concussion will be coming soon, then the wind and firestorm. My poor house, and poor me! I waited and waited. How would I know how long to keep from looking out? After what seemed an eternity, I poked my head up to the window and peeked out between my fingers. Where was the mushroom cloud? I looked again, went outside, and climbed up on the roof, but the sky was clear. Back inside, I turned on the radio and found out that we'd just had an earthquake.

In those moments I had literally been shaken out of my nuclear denial.

I had a vested interest in denying the nuclear threat. In the late sixties I was working on my doctoral dissertation at the University of Southern California, in Los Angeles. My field was innovation theory and technological forecasting—I was almost obsessively interested in the future. At the time, some forecasters were beginning to project a period of declining growth. This worried me. I feared that the need to cut back would create a nasty reaction: instead of gracefully tightening our belts, we in the United States would want more and would pursue reckless growth. Would stock market investors or trade unions be willing to accept limits? Could politicians make decisions that acknowledged limits and still hope to be re-elected? The notion of "more" seemed imbedded in our national psyche. We might even be willing to go to war for more. I envisioned hysteria, social dysfunction, people losing their civility—reactions that would fan the flames of war fever. At some level I knew that if there were a war, it might be a nuclear war.

I led a workshop at San Francisco State that scared me further. The theme was how to teach about the future, and the participants were junior high and high school social studies teachers. They seemed able to look at only the most optimistic, unlimited-growth projections of the future. When I tried to suggest other possibilities, they were visibly uncomfortable. It was inconceivable to them that our standard of living wouldn't keep improving indefinitely. That had been their experience in the past, and they weren't prepared to consider any other scenario. I felt frustrated and discouraged: I couldn't see how to help people explore alternative options for the future. So I put my futures work on hold and focused instead on learning about how people and societies change.

NOT LONG AFTER the earthquake shook me out of my denial, I was invited to join a small study group being formed to figure out how to prevent nuclear war. The other four people in the group were, like me, innovators and achievers. The fact that the nuclear situation hadn't been defused by the efforts of lots of other brilliant people over the past thirty-five years didn't discourage us. We had a can-do attitude; we were going to solve it.

And we had a new approach: we would try to accept the likelihood that at least a few nuclear bombs would be detonated, by accident if not by design. For a long time we had been living in a make-believe world where the possibility of nuclear war did not exist. We were not alone in that fantasy world. Even some of the serious political efforts to prevent nuclear war seemed rooted in denial, relying on frenzied activity to keep the prospect of nuclear destruction out of mind. We reasoned that surrendering our consciousness to the worst scenario might liberate some of the energy tied up in denial. It occurred to us that we were applying the principles of the Japanese martial art aikido—taking the energy of the nuclear threat, going with it, and using the energy against the threat itself.

This approach led us to dream up what now seems like a very strange strategy. We planned to go around the world training firefighters, police, doctors, and other professionals to deal with the aftermath of a nuclear attack. Once these service people moved out of *their* denial and experienced how awful nuclear war would be, we reasoned, the international will to stop the arms race would be aroused. Convinced that this was the approach that would prevent nuclear war, we began meeting every day to prepare ourselves to lead these training programs. Hour after hour, day after day, we pored over technical material on the human and environmental effects of nuclear weapons, watched government films on bomb tests and civil defense procedures, and read analytical essays on deterrence and defense strategies. We immersed ourselves in nuclear war.

The process we went through now appears similar to the invention of homeopathy. When homeopathy was being developed, researchers experimented with consuming small amounts of toxic substances, then watching their bodies' responses. We began to take the nuclear poison into ourselves. As we did, we noticed that our responses fell into several categories:

1. Persistent denial and numbness. We were all reading *The Effects of Thermonuclear War*, a grisly and detailed book put out by the U.S. Government's Office of Technological Assessment. Although I was accustomed to whipping through technical information, I couldn't get through this book. After a paragraph or two my eyes would stop, and blank staring and daydreaming would take over. For awhile we all pretended we were reading the book, but finally we sheepishly admitted to each other we hadn't been able to. It was as if our minds had overload switches.

2. A semi-hysterical mental flailing ("We've gotta do something!"), always followed by a voidy question ("But what will really work?").

3. Absolute bewilderment about how we got into this mess as a human family. ("If I am going to be blown up in an instant, I want to know what happened here.") Where did our human ancestors go wrong? What in our culture allowed us to create a crisis with such high stakes?

4. Fear of losing our dear ones in a nuclear war, and feelings of deep love and connection to all creatures who must live under this terrible threat.

5. A sense some days that small tasks were overwhelmingly meaningless in the face of the nuclear threat. Why vacuum the floor if all life is going to be wiped out? This would be followed by: Why do anything?

6. Plotting, in some dark corner of the mind, how to survive a nuclear war. Investigating civil defense, I was relieved to realize that I lived in the shadow of a hill that might deflect the concussion following a nuclear explosion. If they bombed the weapons storage facilities in Oakland, maybe I'd be safe. But if they bombed the defense industries to the south, I'd be done for. I found myself wondering whether my basement would provide protection from

the blast. I felt glad about all the earthquake preparations I had made.

7. Rage about the nuclear predicament, often directed at military people. One weekend, feeling profoundly disturbed by the nuclear threat, I went to Berkeley, sat in coffeehouses, walked in the woods, and wrote angry poetry:

> Whoever of us remain, let us make a pact
> whoever comes out of the shelters whole and able
> we swear to all the dead others
> we shall go and find them—the men in the brass stars
>   and tin smiles
> and tear them limb from limb.
> They shall not survive the wrath of the survivors.
>   I know I can count on you.
> Set your jaw,
>   narrow your eyes,
>   walk straight in there and shout:
> "The rent on the planet is due, and it's *you*."
> Go for their eyes, their throats
>   and when they are gasping for breath
>   shove it to them in the stomach
>   for the kids and for all our softer selves . . .
> And know that I am proud of you
> Wherever I am . . .

8. Gratitude to the bomb for what it can teach us. By threatening us all, the bomb shows us our commonality and connection. All beings around the world have a common interest in making sure that nuclear war doesn't happen.

9. Curiosity about Soviet people. I wanted to go to the Soviet Union (or at least the Soviet Embassy in San Francisco) and ask people their views of the nuclear predicament; I wanted to meet some Soviet people. But I was afraid of harassment by the U.S. government: would I be suspected of selling secrets? And I noticed my shyness, too, about meeting Soviet people. (I am still working on overcoming this shyness and visiting the Soviet Embassy and Union.)

10. Repeated questioning about strategy. Is there a way to allow nuclear weapons to be used for threatening but not for killing? If a few nuclear weapons are used, can all-out nuclear war be prevented? If global nuclear war is inevitable (after this introductory clause there would be a half-hour digression about whether in fact it was inevitable), then what should we do in the time we have left?

AFTER MEETING for several months, the group decided to spend four full days together to explore the nuclear threat even more intensively. We went to Forest Farm, a beautiful seminar center in Marin County. Fortunately it rained the entire time, so we weren't seduced by the swimming pool or hot tub.

We confessed our fears about exploring the nuclear land inside of us. It felt like the back forty acres of our hearts and minds: wild, out of control, a tangle of overgrown weeds, thistles, and discarded rubbish. We saw several films about nuclear war, talked about them, and heard a lecture from Bob, a physicist in the group, about how nuclear bombs are built and how they work. It didn't seem so hard to create a nuclear explosion, especially if plutonium could be stolen from a nuclear power plant. The more we learned, the worse the situation seemed to us. And as we shared that truth with each other, we felt more vulnerable. Sometimes we found ourselves wishing "they" would do it quickly and get it over with. Other times we wondered whether we were just ruining the time we had left with our obsessive research. We felt empathy for the fanatical hobbyist who escapes into a tiny niche to avoid looking at the big, frightening picture.

John suggested we take turns telling our "nuclear stories"—our life histories as seen through the nuclear prism. I didn't like the idea. What would we say? What would I say? What did nuclear weapons have to do with me?

The nuclear stories turned out to be the most revealing and powerful part of our retreat. People reported having been fascinated with explosives and power, having had nuclear nightmares that had left them helpless for days, having surreptitiously made decisions about where to live based on anticipated fallout patterns. In revealing our secrets we discovered that several of us had friends or relatives who had helped develop the bomb, assembled nuclear weapons, or transported or maintained them. And we had all been paying for them through federal taxes. Nuclear weapons were a hidden member of our family.

Deep in our barely-conscious minds we had been facing nuclear destruction alone for years, and it was eating us up. Now, facing the beast together, we felt immeasurable sadness and anger, terror and hopelessness. It was as though the bomb were going off inside of us, as though we were already nuclear victims. The bomb had exploded on the quality of our lives, threatened our relationships and our confidence in the future. This was a very expensive weapons system!

One night it was Alia's turn. In her nuclear story, she talked about why it was so hard for her to come across the bay to meetings in San Francisco. She was afraid that if there was a nuclear war, and her children were horribly injured, the babysitter would not love the children enough to put them out of their misery. That fear encapsulated the nuclear situation for us. It was the most gruesome thing we could think of. Should we keep poisons or painkillers with us at all times? In the aftermath of a nuclear war, how would we decide whether to use them? We sat together for a long time, crying, talking about our deepest fears for the future.

Then something happened. We started laughing. From deep inside of us a roar erupted as we began wildly to burlesque the situation. We invented nuclear laxatives (to really get things moving). We played with the idea of packing little pieces of nuclear weapons into cereal boxes for children to collect, so that by the time they grew up they could have their own bombs. We considered uses of personal nuclear weapons, like nuking your neighbor for parking in your driveway or for starting a lawnmower at seven o'clock on Saturday morning. As we stood in front of the biggest beast and roared with laughter at its absurdity, our hearts and minds came alive. We had gone through our numbness, we had hit rock bottom, and now we were bouncing up. We stayed awake until 2:00 A.M. Our muscles were weak from laughing.

We awoke the next morning with a new perspective and a sense of renewal; we felt transformed. After months of tiptoeing around the edges of our nuclear darkness, we had faced the terrible truth. And at the core of that truth we had found a part of our humanity that had been choked by our fear. By saying how deeply we feared nuclear war, we had told each other and ourselves how much we loved life. We had said, in effect: "We are passionate human beings!"

There is something about the nuclear threat that says, "You will be destroyed if you face this." Somehow we had walked through that land of terror—and we had survived! The experience filled me with an inner calm and determination. I knew that I had the resources to keep going, to do what was needed to help prevent nuclear war, no matter what my fears.

After the retreat, I began working very hard for human survival. I started developing nuclear comedy sketches with my friend Charlie, traveled around the world to see how people in other cultures viewed the survival crisis, and led workshops similar to the one we had designed for ourselves at Forest Farm.

I HAVE NOW LISTENED to hundreds of people tell their nuclear stories, speaking of their fear, anger, and hopelessness, and of their intense passion for life. I see all of us struggling to tell the truth about living in the nuclear age and, by doing so, to reclaim our lives and the consequences of our collective actions. For if we acquiesce in the death of our planet, then who are we?

A fifteen-year-old student in western Massachusetts eyes me squarely as she says, "I don't have a very long nuclear story, but I want to know one thing. When I dream about nuclear war, why is it always in black and white, and silent?" Overwhelmed by her question, I say nothing.

Another student tells about a dream of the moments just before a nuclear attack. She remembers that a Russian woman lives alone at the bottom of the hill. Not wanting her to face this alone, she goes to be with her.

A third student reports a dream in which the Soviet premier is awakened from a drunken slumber with some news and, without really thinking it through, orders Soviet missiles to be launched. Then, realizing what he's done, the premier shoots himself.

A woman in Colorado says, "I want to promise my children that I'll protect them, and I can't."

A farmer in California's Central Valley breaks down sobbing. For him it is almost a sacred duty to feed his fellow citizens. "If my land and water are ruined," he says, "what will I do? How will I grow anything?"

A Jewish woman who left Germany just before World War II says: "We know that the worst *is* possible."

One day at Sixth Street Park, as Ben and I are discussing the nuclear threat, a hurt look comes over him. "They wouldn't really do that, would they?" he asks.

We each have a direct, ongoing relationship with the survival of the planet. Just as we have family lives, and work lives, and sex lives, now we have "nuclear lives," or "planet-survival lives." I have noticed that my planet-survival life goes in cycles. There is an "outward" part of the cycle, when inspiration is at hand, the focus of my work is clear, and I feel powerful and passionate, ready to call forth all possible resources to increase the odds of human survival.

During the "inward" part of the cycle, denial, powerlessness, and confusion take over. I feel smaller, more overwhelmed, more in touch with suffering. There are some weeks when despair seems to be on every plate, in every dream, in every wrinkle of the fabric of life. I need to sleep more, rest from the struggle, and notice what I'm avoiding thinking about. I read, examine my work, doubt myself. I talk with my friends about what I'm experiencing. I've come to see this part of the cycle as a time of seed-planting. I try to be patient, to value these explorations, to know that in time they may flower into action.

In both parts of the cycle, I see flashes of possible extinction and flashes of life's power. A loud plane overhead sends a chill through me. Is it about to drop a bomb? Driving, I see the panorama of San Francisco and imagine it gone in an instant. Walking among redwood trees that are hundreds of years old, I'm filled with the terror of extinction. I wonder: Do these trees know that their species is threatened *right now*?

The next moment I am overwhelmed by the trees' beauty. The possibility of nothingness reminds me that at one time there was nothing. It makes me feel entirely alive and allied with life. I watch with wonder and appreciation as my chickens lay eggs, tomato plants grow in the garden, a fellow human being tells the heartfelt truth. Like someone sanding her fingertips to make them more sensitive to braille, I sand away my nuclear denial and become more sensitive to the powerful pulls of life and extinction. My own life becomes richer and more intense. And I am forced to wonder: If there were no nuclear threat, would I be able to appreciate life's miracle as fully? Do we as a species need such an immediate and terrible threat in order to value and honor life? To what extent am I attached to this threat and the thrills it brings me?

MY PLANET-SURVIVAL LIFE is one of many questions. I burn to know what it is that has got us into this situation, what will help us get out, and what part of that work is mine. I want to be able to hold these questions so easily and gently that my creativity can address them continuously.

Can we actually uninvent something like nuclear weapons? This was one of the early questions I explored. Then I spent a long time wondering why it was Western civilization that had developed these weapons. I read with excitement about Japan's successful ban on gunpowder in the seventeenth century. But had the ban caused a militaristic reaction that, in the long term, may have been worse? Often even great ideas have unexpected consequences.

What are the effects of nuclear proliferation? Might the mere possession of such a powerful weapon make a leader or a nation more cautious or mature? As less-wealthy countries get nuclear weapons, might they gain a more equitable share of the world's power? Have we finally invented something so disgusting and inconceivably horrible that we will have to learn new ways to share power and resources?

Why has war been developed? Is it a result of the desire for novelty? The need to trade in order to satisfy insatiable desires for variety has caused a lot of trouble. Do wars stem from some countries' meddling in the affairs of others so as to get reliable supplies of resources at artificially low prices? Is it possible to reverse that trend, to reduce the number of things in our lives that come to us at other people's expense? What if we gave up bananas grown on U.S.-owned plantations in Central America? Might that help keep our government from meddling with people there?

I started wondering what in my own life made war more likely. I really love bananas. Would I be willing to give them up if that would reduce the risk of war and put more food on a Central American table?

Are there kinds of international trade that may mitigate against war? If the United States sells grain to the Soviet Union, does that reduce the likelihood of conflict?

Albert Einstein said: "The splitting of the atom has changed everything save our mode of thinking . . ." What are all the ways our thinking needs to change? How do I change my way of thinking? *Can* people decide to change their ways of thinking? How?

Would the key change be to give up defensiveness as an attitude? To stop coveting the lands and resources of others? To stop feeling powerless? To consider the consequences of our actions at every step? Or to see actions and individuals as interconnected rather than as discrete? Sometimes it seems logical to consider this a new time in human history, to start a new calendar for the years after the bomb, and call this year 40 A.B.

ALL THIS PONDERING has helped me make choices in my life and work. Charlie and I continue to perform nuclear comedy. I work with Interhelp, an international network that is helping people break through nuclear numbness and denial. I started a support group for a bunch of people who are doing work for the world. I often help peace groups plan strategy. I spent two weeks in jail for participating in a blockade of the Lawrence Livermore Lab, where nuclear weapons are designed. But I'm still asking questions and not satisfied with my current conclusions. The search is a continuing process, leading me (I hope) to more and more responsible and appropriate behavior in the world. I expect to be fighting nuclear war for the rest of my life, and I hope that's a long time. I now think that it may take four or five generations for our species to learn to make change without war.

Often I think about these things while sitting on the toilet. In the Renaissance, I sometimes imagine, there must have been a woman a little bit like me, trying to make sense out of a very confusing time. What was she thinking about as she sat on the toilet? What were her questions?

Or I picture a woman like me in the Soviet Union, sitting on the toilet, trying to figure out how the Soviets and the Americans can do better, how we can get out of the nuclear predicament.

Or I think of a woman in the future, thinking about the world. What are the questions on her mind as she sits on the toilet? And what does the new design of the toilet look like?

6 | *American Willing to Listen*

INTERNATIONAL TOURISM has never appealed to me. I just can't picture myself staying in a luxury hotel in Rome or Tokyo or Cairo, visiting museums and monuments, scouring gift shops for souvenirs. So for many years, I traveled abroad very little.

But the more I studied the nuclear threat, the more I became consumed with a desire to learn what was happening on this endangered planet, to talk with people around the world and find out how they felt about the future and the nuclear situation. I wanted to enlarge the context of my work to prevent nuclear war. Although theoretically I was fighting for the survival of every human being on the planet, I didn't actually know many people outside the United States. And

73

since I now realized how important it was for me to be connected to the people I was fighting for, my goal became finding people around the world to know and love.

So I sold my house, paid my debts, and bought one of those around-the-world airplane tickets. Actually, the ticket limited me to the Northern Hemisphere, but that was enough for a start.

At my request, friends sent me names of people to talk with and stay with. I planned to go only to cities and towns where I had four or more contacts. After interviewing these contact people, I would ask them to suggest others. But I also wanted to interview people at random. So I came up with the idea of sitting in a park or other public place with a cloth sign that said "American Willing to Listen." Maybe people would come talk to me. I didn't dare tell my friends about the cloth sign for fear that their disapproval, or even their enthusiasm, might crush this fragile, tentative idea.

Before leaving the United States, I drove down to Santa Barbara to test my plan. I interviewed a few contact people there and asked them to refer me to others. And I tried sitting on a park bench with a sign—"Willing to Listen." I felt shy, exposed, and embarrassed. But it seemed better to get a start on those feelings close to home. People did stop and talk, and some of the conversations had depth. This encouraged me.

But on the plane to Japan my doubts and fears resurfaced. What if my interviewing project failed? Perhaps it was a big mistake to try. I had never traveled alone in the world. What if I got sick? What if thieves fell on me? And at the same time I felt excited; I was doing something no one in my family had ever done.

THE PROJECT BEGAN in Kyoto, Japan. First I met my contact people: a Buddhist priest, several environmental activists, and a women's studies class at Kyoto University. It was a few days before I made my "American Willing to Listen" sign and a few more before I got up the nerve to use it. Waiting for a train in Osaka, I said to myself: "If I'm ever going to do this, I should do it here where nobody I know will see me." Unfolding my two-by-three-foot cloth sign, I laid it on the floor in front of me and sat down. Time passed. People came over, sized me up, and walked away. I tried to smile pleasantly. If I busied myself with reading or writing, I was sure that people would not talk to me for fear of interrupting. So I just sat and smiled, all the while thinking, "This is a bad idea. I've spent a lot of money on my plane ticket, and the plan isn't working. I'm making a fool of myself. How will I ever get to talk with ordinary people?"

It was thirty or forty minutes before someone finally stopped to talk—a man in his forties who worked at a shoe factory. He wanted to know what I was doing. I tried to explain but he didn't understand, and I began to fear that I didn't understand either. I was so busy answering his questions that I never managed to ask him any of mine.

After another few minutes, a man of about thirty stopped to chat. He discussed some of his concerns: the border war between North and South Korea over control of rubber trees; consumerism in Japan and the level of consumption in developed countries in general; the investment of massive amounts of Japanese capital in China (he felt a China-Japan alliance might be destabilizing in the region). Closer to home, he was thinking about relations between the sexes. His wife was part of a women's consciousness-raising group, and he and the other husbands had felt jealous of it. They'd tried to start their own group, but it hadn't worked. He was disappointed, and the issue seemed to be unresolved for him.

Boarding the train to Kyoto, I felt happy and relieved. The second man I'd talked with had understood what I was doing and thought it was a great idea. And he had shared a little of his life with me. My confidence grew as the process of meeting people gained momentum. I met people by arrangement and at random, in their homes, schools, and workplaces, as well as in cafés, train stations, universities, and parks. I refined my interviewing technique, asking open-ended questions that would serve as springboards for opinions and stories—questions like "What are the biggest problems you see affecting your country or region?" and "How would you like things to be different in your life?" Being limited to English put me at a disadvantage, but people often volunteered to translate for me.

Early interviews showed me how little I knew about the world. There were vast fields of information that I had never even heard about. For instance, nearly everyone I talked with in Japan mentioned

Kim Dae Jung, a South Korean opposition leader who had escaped to Japan and then been sent back to Korea. I had never thought about relations between Japan and South Korea. In the United States these issues had seemed unimportant and had received only minimal coverage in the news media. Now I was meeting people to whom they were very important. I began to see glimmers of the many ways in which non-Americans saw the world.

It was exhilarating but exhausting. The rapid succession of new issues nearly overwhelmed me—the homogenization of Japanese culture, women's gossip in an Indian village, the flight of capital from Australia to the Philippines and Korea, the aspiration to know God, the near-meltdown of a Japanese nuclear power plant, rural Indian mothers' fears that their children weren't getting enough protein, doubts about the tradition of arranged marriage, regional conflicts over resource and capital allocation, and the frustration of people everywhere who sensed that their destiny was controlled by the superpowers. It occurred to me that I might have to go on interviewing full-time for the rest of my life to get any sense of what was going on in the world.

Four years and hundreds of interviews later, I no longer feel quite so confounded. I'm beginning to get a sense of social and historical currents around the world. On my first world trip I listened to people in Japan, Thailand, India, England, and Scotland. Subsequent trips have taken me to East Berlin, Israel, Palestine, Sweden, and India again. While traveling I've also met people from other countries in Asia, Africa, Latin America, and the South Pacific. My listening project has become a continuing practice, both in the United States and abroad.

ON THE PUNJAB MAIL, a train from Bombay to Hoshangabad, I interviewed the woman who shared my compartment. The wife of a retired railroad worker, she appeared to be in her mid-sixties, and she was traveling with a well-made wooden box that contained a cake for her nephew's wedding. As we rode along she spoke of her worries about her son, a drug addict who was now in Saudi Arabia. The woman's English was quite good, but she had trouble with my name. So I gave her my business card, which identifies me as a futurist. "What's a futurist?" she asked. When I tried to explain, her face lit up. "Oh, you mean a fortune teller?" Preoccupied with getting ready for bed, I wasn't paying much attention. "Sort of," I said. She started asking me about her son. Was he still on drugs? Would he return to India? Or might he marry someone in Saudi Arabia and lose his religion? I said something mildly encouraging about parents and children.

Then she left the compartment. Twenty minutes later she returned, reporting that she had gone through the train announcing that a blue-eyed fortune teller was on board. A group of people had gathered and were waiting to hear their fortunes. She would be happy to translate.

Discovering a line of twenty or thirty people outside our compartment, I tried in vain to convince them of my lack of talent or training in fortune-telling. But they replied, "You gave her a good fortune—you must give us one too." I was up most of the night giving friendly advice and encouragement.

A middle-aged farmer wanted to know about his cow. The cow had been sick, and her milk yield was poor. Would she get better? I asked a few questions and eventually suggested that he consult an animal specialist and get some help. He was grateful for my advice.

A couple came in and asked, "Will we find a husband for our daughter, and will she be happy in her marriage?" I said, "Yes, if they work hard at their marriage, I think they will be happy." They looked at each other with relief. "Will we be able to find her a husband close to our village? We want to have our daughter close to us." As they asked more questions, my translator explained to me about Hindu marriage arrangements. The bride lives with the husband's family, and difficulties can arise if the bride and the mother-in-law don't get along. I suggested to the couple that they interview prospective mothers-in-law to find a cheerful one for their daughter.

Another couple was traveling to visit their grandchild for her first birthday ceremony. Would the granddaughter grow up to be happy, healthy, and prosperous? I tried to get some hints. Was she a healthy baby? I said something mildly encouraging. They said: "In your country you beat children and treat them badly. That's because you don't believe in reincarnation." The woman explained that her beloved mother, who had died a year or two before, had been reincarnated as the baby. So of course this baby was very special to them.

After my stint as the blue-eyed fortune teller of the Punjab Mail, I felt more at home in India. I'd begun to empathize with some of the problems Indians had in their lives. They were worried about their children getting married, just as I had worried about my younger sister's marriage. They were concerned about the health of their parents; I had been through that too.

LISTENING TO PEOPLE, I began to learn how each individual puzzled out large issues from her or his own vantage point. In Varanasi, India, a woman told me that when the Brahmans were thrown out of power in southern India, her husband could no longer find a satisfactory job there. So they moved north to Varanasi. She currently had no job, she said, because Varanasi was a place that didn't respect women. Now she feared that the lower castes would revolt in the north, as they had in the south. Already, she said, "Brahmans are unable to provide strong leadership because they feel so insecure." She expected people to become "more and more selfish, all thinking of themselves, no one thinking of society. And corruption has been getting worse and worse. Corrupt politicians are responsible for the misery in every sphere of life."

In Edinburgh, Scotland, a man who worked with the Scottish nationalist party told me that his country was a colony of England, and England would never grant them independence because the English wanted their offshore oil. The Scots for their part can't mount an effective independence movement, he said, because they are so fiercely individualistic that they can't work together.

In Darjeeling I met a thirteen year old from Bhutan who wanted to become a freedom fighter, to help his region gain independence from China. He earnestly told me about his desire to study hard, to become a strong man, to help his people. I was surprised to see such determination in a person his age.

Two Kyoto women in their twenties were thinking about why Japanese young people were so uninvolved in world affairs. The explanation they had developed was historical: Japanese people had been told that they would win the war against the materialist United States because Japanese spiritual values were superior. So Japan's defeat in World War II was considered a victory for materialism— which the Japanese then embraced. Materialistic, hedonistic values had taken over, they told me, and parents had neglected to give their kids the love and sense of security that would allow them to be involved in larger concerns.

I visited the Rasulia Center near Hoshangabad, where about thirty people—most from the Untouchable caste—live, farm, build bio-gas plants for energy, and work toward self-sufficiency. The leader of the community told me that India's culture used to be one of the greatest in the world—in the forefront in mathematics, art, and religion. India was no longer a leader, he said, because colonialism had squashed the Indians' initiative. In the cycles of history, civilizations rise and fall; India's will rise again. As petroleum becomes more expensive, he projected, societies that are not so dependent on oil (especially less-developed countries) can become a stronger force in the world. He didn't expect that trend to take hold for another hundred years or so, but he was very hopeful about the future and was preparing for it.

A conversation I had with a nuclear engineer in New Delhi lasted six hours. We started out at the YMCA, where I was staying; then he drove me to a fancy club he belonged to, and we ate dinner on the veranda there. We talked at length about nuclear power and his doubts about quality control in India's nuclear power industry. He also helped me understand the fear generated by the state of emergency declared by Indira Gandhi in 1975. Opponents of Mrs. Gandhi's regime were thrown in jail; so when she called an election, people were afraid even to admit to one another that they were planning to vote against her. "When I went into the voting booth," the engineer told me, "I hadn't asked my wife whom she was voting for, and she hadn't asked me. Nobody knew how anyone else was going to vote. Privately we were all afraid that if Mrs. Gandhi won, she would declare another state of emergency and refuse to hold elections in the future. Then we'd never be able to get rid of her." I could see how much he enjoyed being listened to, and how important it was for him to talk about things he hadn't been able to discuss with anyone else.

In all of my conversations, I would look directly at the person I was interviewing and at the same time observe the context we were in—the sounds around us, the birds, the wind, the way people nearby responded to my presence. I would listen to the person as open-heartedly as I could, trying to get a glimpse of the world through his or her eyes. Usually when the conversations lasted long enough, I would start to feel the soft stirrings of a connection— some uncovering of our common root system.

"ARE THINGS GETTING BETTER or worse in your life? In the world?" These questions always got people talking. In Hoshangabad I began to notice that men tended to think things were getting better, while women were generally more pessimistic. A woman to whom I mentioned this observation responded: "That's because the men don't do the shopping."

When I asked about the future, many people went directly to the possibility of nuclear war. Near Kyoto, I spoke with a seventy-two-year-old farmer whose family had lived on the same land since the twelfth century. He feared that the population explosion had made nuclear war more likely. And nuclear war would make it impossible to grow things. "We in Japan are downwind from everyone," he told me.

A Tibetan businessman I met in an antique store offered to take me to "the wisest man in Darjeeling." I followed the businessman through an alley, up a dark staircase, and into a little room. There we met a Tibetan monk, a stout man who sat surrounded by his scrolls. On one side stood an intricately arranged altar; on the other, a window overlooked the Himalayas. The businessman translated as we chatted.

At one point the monk abruptly changed the subject. "What I really want to talk to you about is nuclear war." He reached in among his scrolls, brought out a world atlas, and asked me to show him where Hawaii was. A friend from Hawaii had told him about nuclear war. Since then he had spent a lot of time thinking about it and had come to believe that the root of the nuclear threat was anger. Did I get angry often? he wanted to know. Did people often get angry at me? He advised me that this was an important area to work on. He looked out the window at the sacred Himalayas and mournfully observed, "Nuclear war would ruin these mountains."

A scientist in Varanasi was more sanguine. Nuclear war might solve the population problem, he suggested.

In London, a political activist I met in a bookstore was concerned that the United States would provoke a war in Europe. "You think you can protect your own country by keeping the wars on our continent. Don't you care about us at all?"

I OFTEN ENCOUNTERED hostility toward the United States. A young doctor at the Rasulia Center said, "You Americans have so much and we have so little. Your aid comes with strings attached. You can't give a clean gift; you can't help without getting something out of it, even if it's only a slightly less guilty conscience." Foreign businesses come to India in search of cheap labor, he said. For every dollar they invest in India, they take out three dollars' worth of goods. "That is how you get things cheaply in your country." By now he was yelling. "We don't want your help, your charity, your money! Get your ships out of the Indian Ocean, and get out of our lives!"

Listening to him, I felt personally attacked. I wanted to tell him that I wasn't one of those industrialists. Yet I wasn't wholly divorced from the situation either—I ate cashews from India, and I'd never felt good about food being exported from a hungry country to the United States. So I kept listening, and noticing my own defenses.

A woman in New Delhi said her daughter wanted to know why American protesters did not continue to care about the Vietnamese people after the U.S. troops had gone home. How could we cut the connection so easily? The question stung. As she spoke, feeble excuses ran through my mind. Once our troops had left Vietnam, we no longer had much information about what was happening there.

Anyway, hadn't we done our part by forcing our government to withdraw the troops? Wasn't it time to divorce ourselves from that situation? Even as these defenses arose, I could see I was struggling to convince myself of my own righteousness. But finally I inwardly admitted that there was no justification for my own fickle attention to the plight of the Vietnamese people.

One day I stumbled into the Nonaligned Nations Conference in New Delhi. I stepped into the Oberoi Hotel to make a phone call and then sat down at an unattended desk to write some notes. A woman wearing a brightly-colored dress came up to ask directions. I found out she was from Tonga and asked her to tell me what world issues concerned her most. She expressed outrage about the expansion of the U.S. military base on Diego Garcia, an island in the Indian Ocean. Other delegates I talked with at the conference shared that concern. They were sure that the base would be used for surveillance of southern Asia, northern Africa, and the South Pacific, and would potentially be used as a springboard for military intervention. The woman from Tonga was alarmed that I had no knowledge of any of this. She wanted to know whether my ignorance was typical of the American people. How could I consider myself well-informed and yet know nothing of this important global issue that involved my government?

She offered to bring other people from the conference to talk with me if I would come back in the next few days. So every afternoon I sat down at "my desk" at the Nonaligned Nations Conference. Delegates and others at the conference came to talk with me. The hotel staff began to recognize me and bring me stationery and water.

These conversations gave me a sense of how powerful a force the United States is in the lives of people in Third World nations. They envy the comforts we take for granted and long for a fair share of their own resources and the fruits of their labor. They are afraid of being devastated in a nuclear war they never agreed to take part in. They are bewildered that the American people don't seem to know or care about what is happening in the rest of the world.

I developed two rules for listening to people talk about my country. First, I do not explain or defend the United States. My goal is to see how we look to others and to let that understanding inform my being. Although I continue to feel defensive when my country is criticized, I try to keep listening. Second, I do not divorce myself from criticisms of America and Americans. I do not say or imply, "Yes, some Americans or some parts of our country are that way, but I'm not." I try to take the criticisms to heart.

But it's not only criticisms I encounter. I've also heard out-and-out adoration of the United States. In a park in East Berlin, I met a young couple out for a Sunday stroll. Right away I noticed the American flag pin on the man's shirt. The woman was noticeably pregnant, and both of them had high hopes for the future. They had already applied once for permission to emigrate to the United States, but it had been denied. They had heard all about America from the man's sister, who lives in California, and they longed for the freedom she had told them about. They wanted to work hard, advance in their careers, and be free to buy all sorts of things.

In Varanasi, two women students—one from Iran, the other from Bahrain—told me they knew all about the United States from watching "Dallas" on television. They especially admired the kitchens in "Dallas," and all the electrical appliances. I told them that not everyone in my country had such a high standard of living—that some people didn't even have electricity. I could see they were struggling to believe what I said.

Throughout my travels I met people who had studied in the United States, including many of the delegates at the Nonaligned Nations Conference. Many people spoke of the inequality of the cultural exchange. A woman in Tokyo who had studied at the University of Chicago put it forcefully: "We send our smartest people to your universities to learn from you. But you don't send your students to learn from us. When you come to our country you stay in fancy hotels, go on shopping trips, and travel around in tour buses. There's a lot you miss. Yours is a young society, and you have a lot to learn from us."

I have found people to be grateful and excited that an American has come to learn from them. In Tokyo, Bangkok, Varanasi, and New Delhi, people lined up and sometimes waited for hours to talk with me. Around midnight on the night before I left Varanasi, I was busy packing my suitcase when I heard a knock on the door. It was a Bangladeshi man whom I'd met briefly at the university. He had heard that I was about to leave and he wanted to be interviewed. An engineering student, he was also very interested in international cooperation and wanted to make sure that Bangladesh was represented in my listening project.

I OFTEN ASKED PEOPLE: "What have you learned in your life?" Some had learned about time's constant movement. Others spoke of sorrow and suffering. A revolutionary in Bangkok had learned that "you have to be very careful." He had helped start a people's credit union, but government agents had infiltrated it, shut it down, and confiscated all the money.

Several people said, "It was worth it." They seemed proud to announce that their achievements had been worth the costs. In New Delhi, a woman told me just the opposite. Once a doctor, she had given up practicing medicine. "What good does it do? I get them well but they get sick the next day. They don't have enough food. If I use my medical training, it only means that they are going to suffer longer." So now she makes decorative plaques. I felt threatened by her depression and sense of futility.

ON MY SECOND DAY in Bangkok, I took a taxi driver's recommendation of a place to eat breakfast. The restaurant was a large room with about thirty tables, all but two empty. The only people in the place were two European men at a booth in front, and six or seven Thai women who were sitting or standing around tables nearby. They all looked up as I walked in. I sat in the booth behind the two men and soon got the sense that they were the owners. From a nearby table, a woman looked at me and mouthed the words "I love you." I was so confused I felt like a block of wood. I had come here for breakfast! She gestured to ask if she could join me; I shrugged my shoulders. Another woman came up behind me and started rubbing my shoulders. She said softly, "You want a massage? You want to come up to my room for a massage?" I said, "No, thank you." The first woman scooted around and sat next to me. I tried to carry on as meaningless a conversation as possible. What's your name? Where do you live? I ordered ham and eggs. It was about seven o'clock, so I said to the woman next to me, "You're here early this morning." She said she'd been here late last night too, until 1:00 A.M. She was a short woman, not over thirty years old. She touched my arm with a cold hand—she must have been as scared as I was. Rubbing my arm suggestively, she asked if I'd like to come up to her room. "I can make you very happy." I could no longer escape the conclusion that she was a prostitute who thought I'd come looking for her services.

Putting my hand on hers to stop her from rubbing my arm, I remembered my interview book! I whipped it out and told her I was traveling to learn what was going on in the world. Would she be willing to talk with me? Yes, she would. She told me her job was to sleep with men and let them touch her. She had to work hard to feed her two children. It cost too much to send them to school so they stayed with her mother during the day. The woman's husband had been killed recently when the truck he was driving turned over.

By this time my ham and eggs had arrived, bathed in grease. I couldn't bring myself to eat the food. The other women started coming over to my table, trying to get me to go upstairs with them. I realized what a mystery I must seem: I hadn't eaten my food; I'd just been talking to this woman; perhaps there was something else I wanted that they could give me. Soon, all the women were sitting with us, talking about husbands and children and work and life in Thailand. They spoke of their envy and fear of the American and Japanese business and military men who used their services. Americans are very friendly and have a lot of money, one woman told me, but sometimes when you get them upstairs they're awful.

The women had mixed feelings about the Thai government. A big problem was that houses were being torn down and people were being thrown out of their neighborhoods. The threat of eviction was terrifying. But they did have electric power and lights—that was an improvement over past years.

We talked about children. The women all wished they could send their kids to school, but they couldn't afford the tuition. When I spoke of schooling provided for free by the government, they all started talking at once. What a great idea! I mentioned the school

I'd visited the day before in Bangkok, where poor people could send their children for one baht (about five cents) a day. They hadn't heard of it.

Before leaving I offered the woman who'd first sat with me some money for her time and her teaching. She refused, but I insisted, suggesting she use the money to send her children to the One Baht School.

Still feeling the effects of jetlag, I returned to my hotel room and tried to sleep. But I was too excited. I kept thinking about the Thai women, about how much fun it had been to chat with them, how lively our discussion had been. I thought of what I'd learned about the impact of widowhood. Several of the women I'd talked with had turned to prostitution because they had children to take care of and no husband or other source of support. I could understand their decision, but I fervently wished they had other options. I remembered how an idea that was familiar to me—free public education—had seemed thrilling to them. And I wondered why I had been so afraid in the first moments at the restaurant. What had been so threatening? Of course I had never been propositioned by prostitutes before. What does a decent person do in that situation? I had been unprepared. And yet even in the midst of my fear I had known I was in no real danger. I had to laugh at myself and my fear.

THE NEXT DAY, I returned to the One Baht School to talk more with its founder, Prateep Ungsongtham. A tall, graceful woman in her late twenties, she had founded the school at age fifteen. At the time she had been a childcare worker, and she began to be concerned about the children who brought their younger siblings to her but couldn't afford to attend school themselves. So although she had little schooling herself, Prateep began teaching the older children to read. In exchange they paid her one baht each and helped out with the childcare. Now the school had grown; there were two buildings and a basketball court. Prateep had finished college, and some of her former students who now had college degrees had returned to teach.

The One Baht School is in the middle of Klong Toey, a community of forty thousand squatters. Built on stilts over a canal, their dwellings are made mostly out of found wood but are very clean inside. I found myself wondering: In such terrible situations, where do people get the ideas, the will, and the drive to make things better, not only for themselves but for others? The land is owned by the Port Authority, which at the time was taking steps to evict six thousand slumdwellers in order to build a container port. The school had been a focal point for the efforts against eviction. Prateep said, "To feel secure, we need to know that we can stay here for thirty or forty years."

When Prateep found out that I'd had some experience fighting eviction, she called in the other teachers. It was a Saturday, so there were no classes. Ten of us sat together, and I talked about the International Hotel, the American Indian struggle against uranium mining, and other land struggles. Every now and then our discussion would have to stop because someone would come in with a problem: an old man was dying or a woman's electric bill was forty times what it should be. The teachers were also community workers, and with each interruption one would leave to help resolve the problem.

I dredged up everything I had learned at the I-Hotel about fighting eviction—resistance tactics and techniques from England, China, Japan, the Philippines, and all over the United States. Each idea seemed to suggest others to them, and they would take off in their own language, talking excitedly. They had dreamed of defying the eviction order but had thought of their struggle as an isolated one. Hearing that others around the world had the same dream was exhilarating to them. I had never shared information with a more eager and intensely curious bunch.

DURING MY TIME IN JAPAN, it slowly dawned on me that I had not seen any slums or poor people there. I began asking the people I interviewed where the poor people lived. "We don't have poor people in Japan," I was told again and again. "We are all middle class." Or occasionally, "Oh yes, we have some but I don't know where. Maybe in Tokyo." These answers seemed implausible, so I continued my inquiry. Finally I heard about a district in Osaka called Kamagasaki, where day laborers and poor people lived. Church people from Osaka and Kyoto had organized a night patrol in the area so that people who fell asleep on the street would not freeze and those who were injured could be cared for. Each night of the week a different group was responsible for the watch.

I tagged along with a visiting group from Friends World College. We arrived at a small church in a bleak part of Osaka about 9:00 P.M. Our first job was to check the log books for news of the previous shift. Then the eight of us doing the watch that night gathered our supplies—gloves, first-aid kits, lanterns, and click counters—loaded them into two pull-carts piled high with quilts, and walked to a nearby public building. I was amazed at what I saw there. More than a hundred people were sleeping on cotton mattresses covered with colorful quilts. It was an open-air sleeping center, a 25-by-75-foot area sheltered by the overhang of the building.

We picked up two containers of warm rice balls, put them in our carts, and set out in search of other people who needed a place to sleep. We divided into two teams of four and headed in different directions. As we walked, we found men sleeping in little hidden places. We kept track of how many we came across and where they were sleeping. My partner approached each sleeping person and checked on him. "Good evening. How are you? Are you warm enough? Would you like some rice?" If he was cold, we would give him directions to the sleeping center. If he couldn't walk, we would put him in our pull-cart and take him there.

A toothless old man came up to greet us. His dog followed. The man reminded me of some of my Sixth Street Park friends. To make a place to sleep, he had leaned sheets of plywood against two ramen-noodle carts. He accepted a warm rice ball and chatted with us awhile.

Who are the twenty thousand people who live in Kamagasaki? Most are Koreans (the target of much discrimination in Japan). Others are poor Japanese. Many are men who have left their families. In Japan when you apply for a job, the company looks up your family name in the books of family history. If you do not come from a "good family," or if you are Korean, you have a very hard time getting a job. There are no training programs to help these men. Many are alcoholics. If a man can afford it, he rents a tiny room for about 250 yen (one dollar) a night. At the time of my visit, the landlords had recently doubled their profit by splitting the rooms in half. They would build an additional floor to divide each room horizontally, yielding two cubicles just big enough to crawl into.

At midnight we returned to the sleeping center, where by now about one hundred eighty men were sleeping. Another crew arrived shortly after we did, carrying a man in their cart. They checked his eyes with a light. Each time a new man arrived, a member of the day laborers' union would carry a mattress and quilt to a spot on the ground and make up a bed for him. The worker would tuck the man in, make sure he was warm, and say goodnight. I was moved by the physical contact and the personal care. Workers stay there all night, standing guard so that no one can rob or take advantage of the sleeping men, and covering them up if their quilts slip off. I thought again of the people on Sixth Street in San Francisco, wishing the same kind of care were available to them.

We went back to the church and slept until 5:00 A.M., when we returned to the day labor hall. By that time all the bedding had been put away, and a nearby alley was full of minibuses with signs in their windows advertising for workers—ditch diggers, dirt carriers, and so on. But there were not enough jobs, and two-thirds of the men were left milling around.

At breakfast I interviewed one of the regular watch volunteers. He told me that Koreans have always been badly treated in Japan. They were once slaves, and they still do the lowliest work. Counting the street people is important, he said, because the society doesn't want to acknowledge its poor.

On the train back to Kyoto I thought about poor people and tried to envision better ways to get the world's menial work done. If we had a society where everyone was treated well, who would dig the ditches, pick the crops, and clean the buildings? If the United States didn't have a constant stream of immigrants to do that sort of work, who would do it? Are there ways to distribute menial work more evenly, and to value that work?

EVERYWHERE I TRAVELED, there were aspects of the society that I found disturbing. I tried to notice these, and to see whether my discomfort changed over time. For instance, in Varanasi one of the predominant smells is that of burning cow dung. At first I really disliked it. I lost my appetite and wished I could turn off my nose. To put myself at ease with the smell, I studied the cow-dung cycle. I watched people gather the dung, mix it with a little dry grass, and slap it onto a nearby wall. There is hardly a vertical surface that isn't adorned with dung patties clearly imprinted with the hand of the patty-maker. The dung is left to dry and later plucked off and either burned or sold. This is the fuel most poor people use to cook and keep warm. Some patty-makers have a design sense and cover the walls in an artistic fashion; others seem to slap it up without thought or plan. As I became better acquainted with the process, the people, and the city, the smell bothered me less and less until the discomfort finally left entirely.

To this day I cringe at the cultural faux pas I know I've made in my world travels: eating with my left hand in India, touching a Brahman friend on the shoulder as I bade him farewell, losing track of which slippers were for which room in the home of a Japanese host. There must have been dozens of blunders that I still don't realize I made. I have learned to ask my hosts to forgive me for any disrespect I may have inadvertently shown for them, their religious practices, or culture.

WHEN I RETURNED from my world trip, I also returned to my job at Sixth Street Park. In a staff meeting some of the guys asked me to tell them what I had learned. I said I had been struck by the poverty in Japan, Thailand, and India. I told them I had seen people in Bombay living like animals, and people with severe disabilities out foraging for food on their hands and knees. Bird, who was sitting directly across the table from me, looked at me squarely, with a tear in the corner of his eye. He said, "It broke your heart, didn't it?" I could tell that even though he was very poor by the standards of the society around him, he had seen poverty much worse—maybe in the service or the merchant marine—and it had moved him. The park staff talked of their relative good fortune and of the idea of starting an international union of down-and-out people that could go on strike for better treatment.

It used to be that when I thought of India, I'd imagine the outline of the country on a map. I'd think of hungry people, women in saris, wild animals, mysticism, gurus—just floating impressions. Now I know what India looks like, smells like, feels like. I know some Indian people and have seen how their lives work in their own environment. I have a sense of some of the unresolved issues in the lives of individual people there.

This perceptual shift reminds me of going on field trips with my college zoology professor, Dr. Stanford. He would take us to an open field that didn't look special or interesting to us. Then Doc Stanford would say, "Let's take a look at just this one square meter." We'd explore its ecology in detail—the grasshoppers and beetles, the lichens and grasses, the parasites growing on the stalks of plants. Three or four inches below the surface, we'd find worms and a new set of bacteria; further down there were fungi growing on the roots of plants. We'd measure the acidity of the soil and note the kinds of plants it supported. We'd study the wind patterns, the geology, how water percolated down through the soil. We could take hours studying a square meter.

And that's the way I feel about the world now. I used to picture the world as a globe with continents and oceans and countries painted orange, yellow, and pink. Then, when I saw photographs of the earth taken from space, I saw a living whole. Now I see life on that spinning ball: specific places, specific concerns, specific lives.

I'm continually thinking of the people I've met around the world. That couple on the Punjab Mail: Is their granddaughter growing up healthy and strong? How are the street people in Kamagasaki doing? Have the squatters near the One Baht School successfully resisted eviction? In August I think about the monsoons in India. I can see the waters of the Ganges rising.

My listening project is a kind of tuning–up of my heart to the affairs of the world. I hear the news in a very different way now, and I act with a larger context in mind. Conspicuous consumption has become more difficult now that I have met poor people around the world. I hold myself accountable to the people whose lives I have seen. And I work to keep nuclear war from happening to us all.

I carry with me the pain of some of my partners in the world, but it does not weigh me down. Much of my life and environment have been designed to isolate me from this pain, but I have come to see it as a kind of holy nectar. The more I drink, the more I can taste what is happening on this planet.

7 | *Would You Do This to Your Mother?*

IN THE SUMMER OF 1980 I heard a speech that changed my thinking. American Indian Movement co-founder Russell Means described capitalism and socialism as more alike than different. Both systems sprang from European civilization; both, he said, are wedded to the European "despiritualization" of the universe. Capitalist and socialist countries are industrial societies, out of touch with the forces of nature; both have decimated indigenous peoples.

He traced environmental problems to the European view of land in terms of its utility to the industrial economy. "The mountain becomes gravel, and the lake becomes coolant for a factory."

In the European system of "development," individuals and

companies can own more land than they can responsibly care for. Means sketched out an alternative: a land-based political philosophy that would give decision-making power regarding the land to those who live on it, care for it, and have a direct stake in its long-term well-being.

The talk Means gave was part of a week-long "Survival Gathering" of American Indians, ranchers, and environmentalists in the Black Hills of South Dakota. The land-based idea struck a chord with many of us there. The concepts were exhilarating; hundreds of people sat up discussing them long into the night. Certainly executives sitting in the Bank of America headquarters in San Francisco shouldn't make decisions about pesticide use on farms hundreds of miles away! They have no direct relationship to the full range of costs. If their families aren't breathing air thick with pesticide spray and aren't drinking water poisoned by chemical residues, they are more likely to base their decisions on abstract economic considerations. Observing that industrial corporations seemed particularly prone to this kind of irresponsibility, I began to wonder: How can we evolve industrial forms that are more connected to those who pay the human costs of development?

Means had talked primarily about the Indians and their need to control the Black Hills land they'd been given by treaty, but I could see urban applications of his idea as well. The International Hotel struggle and the establishment of Sixth Street Park were essentially land-based campaigns. If someone else has control over your home and wants to turn it into a parking lot, you cannot shape your own destiny.

The land-based idea has become a new frame of reference for me. It has helped me understand the relationship between human beings and our natural environment: in reflecting on my own experiences of environmental degradation, in hearing the story of a pioneering anti-pollution battle in Japan, and in working with a campaign in India to clean up the Ganges River.

I GREW UP loving the Idaho land. How could I help standing in awe of this planet, as I watched seeds planted in the dark, rich volcanic soil grow into food and flowers? I loved the trees, the sagebrush that smelled so fragrant after the rain, the powerful Snake

River with its splendid canyon, even the dark, unbroken lava rock, fifty miles south of Twin Falls, that looked like the surface of the moon. I loved swimming and rowing around Pettit Lake in the summer; the water was so clean that we just brought it in buckets from the pier for drinking. I loved floating for hours on inner tubes down the Salmon River among the glorious Sawtooth Mountains.

But I also remember the dredged rivers I saw when I was young. Our family used to enjoy exploring Idaho ghost towns on vacations. Several times we came upon rivers whose banks were piled high with rocks and sand. Although the rivers were still flowing, nothing grew alongside them. They looked ugly and vandalized. My father told us that miners had dredged for gold and silver. They had come with big machines that had chewed up the river and spit the gravel out along the banks—and they hadn't even tried to restore it. Everyone in the family was outraged. We were seething as we drove along those rivers. Finally my father stopped taking us along that route because what we saw upset us so.

I remember the Fish & Game Department's efforts to get trout into Pettit Lake. We already had plenty of good fish in the lake. We had redfish, rare landlocked salmon that are fun to catch and delicious to eat. We had minnows, suckers, and whitefish. But the Fish & Game men wanted trout, and they decided the reason there were no trout was that they didn't have places to live in the lake. So they cut down some trees, wired them together, wired some rocks to the trees, and then sunk the trees in the lake to provide homes for the trout.

That didn't work.

Years later, the Fish & Game men came up with a new idea. They waited until fall, when all the redfish had left the lake, and planted depth charges to explode the suckers and whitefish—which they figured were eating the trout. Swarms of dead fish floated to the top of the lake and down the outlet.

That didn't work either.

Still there were no trout. There were no redfish in the lake for a few years. The suckers and whitefish were gone, too.

No one who loved the lake would have sunk trees in it, or planted depth charges. The people who made that decision didn't live near the lake; they weren't constantly reminded of the consequences of their actions.

In the mid-seventies I started a bee farm with some friends in Watsonville, California. We thought Watsonville would be a perfect place to keep bees because there were apple orchards all around: the bees could collect nectar from the apple blossoms. But strangely, our bees started to die. The pile of dead bees grew outside the hives; soon they were all dead.

At the county agricultural extension office we told an agent what had happened. He said that the orchard owners had been spraying chlordane, an insecticide, to protect their apples from bugs. Our bees must have been in the apple blossoms during the spraying, and the chlordane had poisoned them. (The reason the growers spray chlordane, I later found out, is that the Agriculture Department grades apples based on lack of insects. They take random apples and if they find insect damage, they downgrade the apples. Apple growers have to make sure their fruit is insect-free to get a grade A rating. So they overspray: better to put on too much than not enough.)

There seemed to be nothing we could do; I was furious. We had gone to great lengths to make our farm organic; we'd even gotten untreated seeds for our vegetable garden. We didn't feed our chickens anything except day-old bread from the health food bakery. And our bees were dying from chlordane! Some days we could smell chlordane in the air. What was it doing to *us*?

When the Three Mile Island accident happened in 1979, I had already been protesting nuclear power and had no illusions about nuclear safety. Still I was outraged: the utility company and the Nuclear Regulatory Commission were trying to reassure us instead of trying to protect us. And I was scared because I knew that if the groundwater gets irradiated, then well water becomes unsafe, and springs for hundreds of miles around become contaminated. There wasn't much discussion of that. I still shudder at the thought of what a meltdown would do to the groundwater. I am filled with repulsion and shame to think that our overconfident attitude toward technology could allow us to ruin the land and water for generations to come.

And I remember hearing about radiation damage among the Diné, a Navaho people. At the Survival Gathering I attended a workshop led by a Diné woman in her forties. "I want you to look at this," she said, holding out a sheaf of papers an inch and a half thick.

Diné men had been working as uranium miners, and she had suspected that their exposure to radiation was causing health problems. Although she had no training as a researcher, she had taken it upon herself to investigate. She went from house to house on the reservation, interviewing the women about stillbirths, miscarriages, birth defects, the incidence of cancer, and other health problems. "There's hardly a family that hasn't suffered from these health problems," she said. "This is what's happening to my people." I'll never forget that woman's determination to see that this suffering be acknowledged and stopped.

SOMEHOW, OUR ECONOMIC SYSTEMS have allowed the human and environmental consequences of economic development to be ignored. Corporations decide to mine uranium without considering the suffering of the miners; the nuclear power industry fails to think through the waste and leakage problems inherent in the technology. How is it that people who are otherwise intelligent fail to act intelligently on behalf of the common good? Something must disconnect. Some wires must come loose. I don't know of any economic system that deals adequately with long-term consequences. Russell Means makes me wonder: Can we develop forms that *do* promote social responsibility?

And what relationship do I have to the degradation of the environment? When I lived in Los Angeles, this question was laid out in all its complexity. At first the smog shocked me: I looked toward the mountains and saw beige air. When I left the city for a few days—long enough to get used to air that didn't smell foul—coming back to Los Angeles was particularly jarring. Some days there were smog alerts on the radio: the air was so bad that kids weren't allowed to play in the schoolyard, because they would breathe too much of the polluted air while running around.

I knew I was contributing to the problem by driving my car, but what could I do? Years before, General Motors had bought up Los Angeles's public transit system and dismantled it—now there was virtually no way to get around that sprawling city except by automobile. I tried to live near my work and to drive as little as possible. Eventually I moved back to San Francisco, where the daily effects of my car exhaust were less visible, less disturbing, but no less damaging to the environment.

If we are serious about being environmentally responsible, it will take collective as well as individual changes. We will need to alter radically both our personal habits and some of our society's arrangements.

Every time I hear about another toxic dump, I wonder what products I use whose manufacture required those chemical wastes. When I reach for a piece of beautiful, bug–free fruit, am I voting for the continued use of chlordane in the orchards?

SEVERAL MONTHS after the Survival Gathering, my American Willing to Listen project took me to Japan. A friend there introduced me to Aileen Smith, a wonderfully engaging woman of thirty. When our interview began I had no inkling that her life had been dramatically changed because of a major environmental battle.

Aileen's father was American and her mother Japanese; she had lived alternately in Japan and in the United States. Now she was on Christmas vacation from New York University, where she was studying environmental health. She told me that although she felt emotionally connected to the Japanese people, they ostracized her because of her mixed parentage.

After we had talked for some time, Aileen casually mentioned a book called *Minamata*, which she had written with her late husband, American photojournalist W. Eugene Smith. I was intrigued. The book documented a citizens' struggle to overcome the effects of industrial pollution in Minamata, a fishing and farming town on the southern Japanese island of Kyushu.

In the early 1950s, Aileen told me, residents began to suspect that something was wrong. They noticed fish floating on the sea; then shellfish, birds, cats, and other animals showed strange symptoms. Soon townspeople began to fall ill: limbs and lips tingled and became numb; speech slurred; motor functions went out of control. Some people died. Children were born disabled. In 1959 mercury poisoning was identified as the cause. The mercury was reaching the population through fish, which had been contaminated by chemical wastes discharged into Minamata Bay by the Chisso Corporation.

Aileen and Eugene Smith lived in Minamata for three years in the 1970s, documenting the lives of victims and their families and the multifaceted struggle for financial compensation and social responsibility. Victims repeatedly told the Chisso Company: "The question is not whether you can or cannot pay; you are responsible for paying. You *must* take care of what you have done, to the end."

Eventually, the Kumamoto District Court ordered Chisso to make indemnity payments to a group of "verified victims." The 1973 verdict stated: ". . . In the final analysis . . . no plant can be permitted to infringe on and run at the sacrifice of the lives and health of the regional residents . . . The defendant cannot escape from the liability of negligence."

A year earlier, during a peaceful demonstration outside Chisso's corporate headquarters, men hired by Chisso to do strong-arm duty beat up several Minamata Disease victims and smashed Eugene against the pavement, crushing several vertebrae. He died several years later as a result of those injuries. Talking with Aileen, I got a sense of the magnitude of the costs of environmental destruction. Not only had the people of Minamata suffered from the poisoning, but their campaign had taken a heavy toll. For Aileen the price had included her husband's life.

Hearing this story, I realized I was listening to someone who had helped win a victory for the whole planet. She and the people she worked with in Minamata had set an example. They had shown how ordinary people could turn a terrible situation around and force a company to take responsibility, to deal with the consequences of its actions. I asked Aileen, "Have you ever told your professors at NYU that you helped document one of the first recognized cases of health damage from industrial pollution?"

"They never ask what the students have done," she told me.

The suffering that arises from environmental pollution is borne by individuals. But for change to occur, that suffering must be made visible so the community can say, "This is ours." In Minamata the first step in the townspeople's campaign was to acknowledge to each other what was happening. In the fifties, when the first human effects of the poisoning were cropping up, no one knew the cause. "Minamata Disease" was believed to be contagious; one shopkeeper would take money from victims only with chopsticks. Many people tried to hide their ailments or pretend they were healthy. Divisions arose between the healthy and the sick.

But as long as they hid their suffering, they were powerless. For many people, "going public" was the most difficult step: they had to give up the pretense that nothing was wrong, that their families were all right. Only then was it possible to determine the patterns of the problem and to assign responsibility.

MY AMERICAN WILLING TO LISTEN project also took me to Varanasi, India, where I learned of the serious pollution problems of the Ganges River. The city of Varanasi, also known as Benares, snuggles up to the Ganges River, and it was there that I met Dr. V.B. Mishra, a friend of a friend in the United States. A humble, graceful man, Dr. Mishra is a professor of civil engineering at Benares Hindu University. He is also the *mahant* (hereditary priest) of one of Varanasi's chief temples and is respectfully addressed as "Mahantji." Since adolescence he has practiced one of the strictest forms of orthodox Hinduism. Isolated from his peers by their reverence for him, he is attracted to Westerners who talk freely with him, tease him, and treat him as an equal.

Ganga (called Ganges by the British) is worshipped by the Hindus as mother and goddess. They call the river "Ganga Ma"— Mother Ganga—and they see it as the source of everything they have.

It was easy for me to understand this veneration. I grew up loving the beautiful Snake River. Its size and force never let us delude ourselves into thinking we human beings were omnipotent. My father used to say, "Everything we have comes from the Snake." All the wealth in Idaho's Magic Valley came from farming, and all the farms were dependent on the river's water for irrigation. No matter whether you sold shoes or insurance, your livelihood depended on the Snake. The level of the water table was a topic of constant discussion.

We drew our electricity from dams along the river: one at Shoshone Falls and one at Twin Falls. My grandfather managed the utility district for Idaho Power Company, and he often took us to the falls for picnics and swimming.

The Ganga plays an even greater role in people's lives than does Idaho's Snake. The most devout bathe in Ganga every day—not just to wash but to fulfill a religious obligation and to express devotion.

Hindus regularly take small brass pots to the river, fill them with water, and place them on the altars in their homes. High stone steps, called ghats, line the western bank to provide approaches to the river and to protect Varanasi from floods during the monsoon season.

Ganga is a beautiful, wide, slow-moving river, with fresh-water porpoises playing in its waters. But the river's blemishes are also immediately apparent. Although Hindus consider it holy, and although the Indian people are very conscious of personal hygiene (they even have a special implement for cleaning the tongue), they have allowed Ganga to become badly polluted. I was revolted to see people sweep their hands along the top of the water, removing the feces floating there in order to clear a place to bathe or drink. I would often see the corpse of a buffalo or a person floating down the river.

Mahantji loved the river and told me he wished something could be done to heal it. I told him about some of the ecological campaigns I knew of in the United States. But he saw no hope for Ganga. The day I left Varanasi, I went for a last walk along the riverbank. I felt the way I had felt at the end of a visit with my aging grandmother—maybe she would die before I saw her again. I wanted to remember this lovely river.

A SERIES OF SMALL MIRACLES brought Mahantji to the United States. He met with Pete Seeger and other members of the Clearwater Project, a group that has made significant progress toward cleaning up the Hudson River. In San Francisco, Mahantji and I talked about the extent of the changes that would be necessary to save the Ganga. As with the Minamata campaign, the connection between people's suffering and water pollution would need to be drawn; unquestioned habits and policies would need to be changed. Mahantji voiced a personal concern: Would he be able to take on the responsibilities of cleaning up the river and still remain a traditional Indian? Would his involvement in the campaign force him to compromise his religious practices? In spite of his fears, I knew there could be no one more appropriate to launch this campaign than Mahantji. As a respected spiritual leader and academician in Varanasi, he could lead a campaign that would be accepted in both communities. At Mahantji's request, I agreed to come to India for a month in each of the next five years to help develop a strategy to clean the Ganga.

ONE OF THE OLDEST living cities on earth, Varanasi is also considered by many to be India's holiest. For thousands of years it has been a center of Hindu philosophical discourse. According to Hindu mythology, the god Shiva selected Varanasi as his home on earth, and saints have seen the city as a column of light. Pilgrims from all over India travel to Varanasi. The lifelong desire of religious Hindus is to have at least one holy dip in the sacred river before they die. Many come to await their death. It is considered particularly auspicious to die in Varanasi and have one's ashes placed in the Ganga; many people believe it ensures salvation.

Bodies are cremated at a burning ghat on the riverbank. The ashes don't pose much of a pollution problem, but many people cannot afford enough wood for a thorough cremation. So they buy as much as they can, then dump the partially burned corpse into the river. When people die in the local hospital, orderlies are given a little money for wood and told to take the bodies to the burning ghat. But all too often the orderlies dump the bodies off the bridge at the end of town and pocket the money. These bodies float down the river, pushed by the current toward the populated bank. Dead buffaloes, cows, and other animals are also dumped into the river, to float until they are eaten by dogs and vultures. As custom dictates, bodies of holy people and those who have died of infectious diseases are not cremated, but are wrapped in cotton, weighted with rocks, and deliberately sunk in the river.

The Benares Hindu University campus, at the upstream end of Varanasi, houses over fifty thousand people. An open channel carries the untreated sewage from the university and the upstream part of the city directly into the river. A bend in the river holds the sewage against the city-side bank of the river. One hundred yards downstream a pumping station draws the city's supply of drinking water; its intake pipe draws water from the edge of the river where the concentration of sewage is highest.

As the river flows beside Varanasi, other open ditches discharge sewage into the river along the same bank where people bathe and wash their clothes, dishes, and animals. On an upper level of the ghats men defecate and their feces are swept by ghat caretakers into the river.

Although the most massive pollution problems are caused by

human sewage and corpses, there are industrial waste problems as well. A diesel locomotive factory, also upstream from Varanasi's water intake, discharges mercury and corrosive acids directly into the river. And a paper factory further upstream injects its noxious chemicals into the river. Cities to the north also contribute both industrial waste and human sewage. Water samples from the Ganga have turned up arsenic, mercury, lead, and other heavy metals. The Indian government is planning to build a large "industrial colony" on the Ganga, five miles upstream of Varanasi. And a nuclear power plant is under construction in Narora, a small town further upstream.

The headwaters of the Ganga are high in the Himalayas, and the water is exceptionally rich in dissolved oxygen because it drops from such a height. The more oxygen it contains, the more biological matter a river is able to break down. Most Indians believe that Ganga can purify herself. Although this seems to have been true for many years, the pollution is now too severe.

Serious gastrointestinal problems plague the population, particularly children. In Varanasi, gastrointestinal illness is the leading cause of death among children (in the United States, it is automobile accidents). If the river were cleaner and the odds of children's survival to adulthood were greater, families could eventually have fewer children, and their lives could be more stable. (The United Nations has found that when the infant mortality rate drops significantly, the birthrate drops within two generations.)

The pollution of the Ganga is so serious that it has even begun to affect Mahantji's religious practices. Temples like his traditionally dispose of thousands of *malas* (flower garlands) every day by dumping them in the river. But Mahantji has changed his temple's practice: the malas are now buried. And although Mahantji's daily devotional practice calls upon him to sip Ganga water three times, he has reluctantly stopped doing this. Almost nothing can cause a devout Brahman to break such traditions.

WHEN I ARRIVED in Varanasi to begin my work with the Swatcha Ganga ("Clean the River") project, I made appointments with each of the seven men on the the board of directors to hear their thoughts on the campaign. After each interview, I'd ask, "Who else should I interview about Ganga?" They sent me to a pathologist who studies illnesses resulting from water pollution, a priest who sings religious songs about the river, a boatman, an insurance salesman, a surgeon at the university, and the Maharaja. Initially, I interviewed more than twenty people.

I asked each person what had been the most important changes they had seen in their lives. All but the youngest people told me of India's independence struggle and what it had been like for them. In terms of local changes, they focused on scandals, thefts from temples, construction projects, the increasing availability of consumer goods, and people dying. I also asked how they could tell when a change was going to happen, so that I could get a sense of what they considered to be significant milestones. Finally, I asked questions that related directly to the project: What stories can you tell me about the Ganga? How has Ganga changed? Why is it important to clean up the river? What can ordinary people do to protect Ganga?

From my interviews, I found that there was a tremendous disparity in factual information among people working to save the river. Someone told me that the water department never treated the water taken from the river for drinking. Others said that the department put two or three chlorine tablets in the water each week. Another person told me, "When the government can afford it, they put in chlorine tablets. If the tea tastes bad, you know they're treating the water. Our tea rarely tastes bad." Clearly, research and education were needed on this subject so that people could have a more accurate picture of the situation.

Early on, I learned that I must take care not to insult a river that the people worship. It would be a major error to insinuate that the river was not perfect. So I would say, "The Ganga is a holy river. How have you come to terms with the fact that it's polluted?" I carefully probed to find out how I might present difficult information about the river in ways that would be culturally acceptable and respectful of people's beliefs. One day someone in the campaign said, "The river is holy, but it is not pure." Statements like this helped guide me in my exchanges with people.

To uncover some strategies for the campaign, I tried to discover focal points for concern about the Ganga. "What is it that pains you most about the river?" I would ask. Were people disturbed most by the corpses floating in the river? The lack of sewage treatment?

The use of soap for bathing and washing clothes? The disrepair of the existing precautionary systems?

Everyone mentioned the children and the drastic effects of water-borne diseases on them. So in my interviews, I began asking, "How are you preparing your children to take on the cause of the river?" Cleaning the river will take a long time; people who are now five and ten and fifteen years old will have to carry it on. And getting children involved might also increase their parents' awareness.

One day, several leaders of the project burst in to tell me about a great idea they'd just had: a poster contest for local children to depict the pollution of the river. That year we took a slide show about Ganga into more than a dozen schools, and hundreds of children drew pictures of the river for the contest.

As my interviews continued, new questions arose. For example, it struck me as odd that all the key people in the Swatcha Ganga movement were men, so I began asking, "Where are the women in the campaign?" When I asked this of a woman whose husband was a board member, she volunteered to bring a woman friend over to discuss it. We had tea, talked, and decided to call a larger meeting. This time there were twenty women, and they decided to organize a women's conference about the Ganga. Two months later, more than four hundred women came to a *shamiana* (a brightly colored tent), erected on the banks of the Ganga, to hear about the pollution of the river. (The turnout was beyond our expectations, and over two hundred women signed up to participate in future organizing work.)

One effect of my listening process was that the people I interviewed could see that the problems with the river were important to people from far away. Leela, a former secondary school principal who had become a central figure in the Swatcha Ganga campaign, often used my presence to shame others into working on the project. When we went on speaking engagements together, she would point to me and say, "Here is someone who has traveled all the way from the United States to help save the river. How can you, who live here and love the river, do nothing?" (My efforts to dissuade her from using guilt to motivate people were futile.)

THE SWATCHA GANGA CAMPAIGN has identified many of the changes needed to save the river. Sewage must be properly treated; corpses must be completely cremated; people must refrain from washing with soap in the river and defecating on the ghats. Temples must stop disposing of *malas* in the river, and industrial pollution must be brought under control. To reduce flooding, the deforestation of the Himalayas must be reversed. (Clearcutting on the Himalayas' steep slopes causes tremendous erosion, and large amounts of silt raise the water level, exacerbating flood conditions.)

Saving the river will require designing and building public toilets and bathing facilities that will be a clean and attractive alternative to current practices; researching alternative methods of cremation that are inexpensive, thorough, and not dependent on wood; pressuring the city and university to build sewage treatment plants that use appropriate technology; and pressuring the Indian government to set strict pollution standards for industry.

The goal of the Swatcha Ganga campaign is to build a social climate that will enable these changes to happen. It would not be enough to build sewage treatment plants, make laws against dumping *malas* and corpses, and so forth. A law prohibiting dumping corpses in the river is no more effective than people's ability and commitment to live within that law. (In fact, there is an unenforced regulation that prohibits the dumping of corpses except at certain "control points" along the river; government boats are supposed to pick up the corpses at these points and make sure they are burned.)

To ensure that bodies are not dumped in the Ganga, a fundamental shift of consciousness will be necessary. It must become socially unacceptable to dump a corpse into the river. In that climate, anyone dumping a corpse would be subject to criticism and ostracism. I saw this kind of shift occur in California during the drought in the late seventies. Being an upstanding citizen began to include conserving water; having a green lawn reflected antisocial behavior. So, as we work toward technical and legal solutions to the Ganga's problems, our fundamental goal is to allow people to change their relationship to the river.

People's relationship to the Ganga is born of habit. It hasn't been rethought for many generations. For hundreds of years, parents have been taking their children to the river, teaching them their religious devotions and other daily routines. We are asking people to re-evaluate this relationship, to question the belief that Ganga will purify herself, and to begin to see that just as Ganga takes care of them, they must be her caretaker too.

THE SWATCHA GANGA'S public information campaign uses many familiar techniques, including speeches and slide presentations for schools and civic groups, posters, conferences on the scientific aspects of the problem, and lobbying of government leaders. On holy days, when huge crowds flock to the river, Swatcha Ganga people board a houseboat strung with banners and distribute leaflets on the bank.

During my most recent visit, the campaign sponsored a cultural festival featuring poetry reading one night and folksinging the next. The theme was pollution of the Ganga, and local artists were called upon to write special material that grappled with the issue. Standing room—only crowds of fifteen hundred attended the events, listening intently until three or four in the morning. One folksong was particularly moving to the audience, and I asked my friend Uma to translate it for me. "The mother is alone in her suffering. Even though she is ill, her only thought is: If the mother is sick, how can the children be strong?"

The consciousness-changing campaign is beginning to show tangible results. Recently the Indian government allocated hundreds of thousands of rupees for construction of sewage treatment plants along the Ganga; Prime Minister Rajiv Gandhi has made saving the river one of his highest national priorities.

Toward the end of my visit in January 1985, I started hearing people say, "The river looks cleaner." They speculated it was because the sewage pumping stations built in 1972 were finally working. The World Bank had spent millions of rupees to construct a lateral sewer line with five stations to pump untreated sewage beyond the city—where a sewage treatment plant is to be built. But, after considerable investigation in the early days of the Swatcha Ganga campaign, it had come to light that these pumps had never worked.

Two city agencies were responsible for the project—one in charge of operations, the other in charge of repairs. When questioned, each agency blamed the other for the problem. The head of one agency had visited Mahantji several times to persuade him to stop talking about the pumps. The official insisted that they simply couldn't be made to work and offered technical information to support this position.

But since my previous visit, the bureaucratic will had somehow been found to replace this official with a man who promised to get the pumps running. I hurried off to visit the two pumping stations that had begun operation. I heard the whirring of the motors, saw the water surging through, felt the vibrations of the pumps. They were really working! The city's sewage would no longer be contaminating its own drinking water supply; people would be ingesting fewer vitality-sapping intestinal parasites. I danced down the stairs of the pumping station.

BEFORE LEAVING VARANASI at the end of my first one-month spell of work there, I invited my friends to a farewell party at the headquarters of the Swatcha Ganga campaign. On the night of the party people poured in, everyone dressed in their best. The women sat on one side of the room, the men on the other. I had invited friends from all castes and classes—which is not a common practice. The servants who came were reluctant to sit down and did so only with considerable encouragement. I served chocolate pudding, made from a mix I'd brought from the United States, as well as some local sweets.

At my urging we all introduced ourselves in turn, mentioning something good that was happening in our lives. I had promised them some comedy, since many knew I was a comedian in another part of my life. So I told some funny stories about my time in India. Mahantji, Uma, and others translated.

Then I explained that I had begun my work for social change in the civil rights movement, whose leader, Martin Luther King, Jr., had taken many of his lessons from Mahatma Gandhi. I told them how important Gandhi's ideas of nonviolence had been in my thinking and development. Now I was in India, where much of my inspiration had come from, so in effect I was their grandchild. I invited them to sing a song from the United States that had been used since the civil rights movement to express commitment and determination. The fifty of us stood in a circle and sang "We Shall Overcome" in Hindi, concluding with a newly composed verse: "We Shall Clean the River."

8 | The Human Family at Its Worst

THE FIRST TIME I heard there was to be an international conference on holocaust and genocide, I knew I had to go. As I worked to prevent nuclear war, I was reminded that millions of people had already faced holocaust. What could those who had endured such horror teach us about facing the threat of global annihilation?

I flew to Israel in June 1982, shortly after the Israeli invasion of Lebanon. The week-long conference was held at the Tel Aviv Hilton, on the Mediterranean shore. Most of the several hundred participants were Jewish survivors of Nazi concentration camps, and many were now Israeli citizens. There were also people who had protected Jews during the war, as well as people who had been hidden, children of survivors, and scholars of holocaust and genocide.

IT HAS TAKEN FORTY YEARS for survivors to begin talking openly about what happened during Hitler's regime. And at the conference I learned that the Nazi holocaust was not the only one in this century. Armenians described the atrocities committed against their people by the Turks between 1915 and 1922. A man from Tibet said that the Chinese had killed hundreds of thousands of his people from the 1960s to the present. Accounts were given of holocausts and genocides against gypsies, Cambodians, Australian aborigines, and indigenous peoples throughout the Americas.

Although the participants disagreed about what constituted holocaust, there was consensus that this century is unique in the magnitude of suffering inflicted by human beings on other human beings. No one knows why this has occurred on such a massive scale in our time. But it seems clear that a key prerequisite for holocaust and genocide is dehumanization. Victims must be portrayed as less than human (as when, during the Vietnam War, Americans were told that Asians didn't value life as highly as we did). Perpetrators of holocaust and genocide are dehumanized too; they must subjugate their innate connection with other human beings to the principle of "saving the Aryan race" or "protecting national interests." Such systematic dehumanization seems to be at the root of what makes massacre possible.

Researchers at the conference suggested that empathy mitigates against holocaust and genocide. Traditional safeguards such as laws and social institutions have not proved adequate, they warned. Every society that has committed genocide has done so in violation of its own laws. I learned that people at the United Nations Human Rights Commission are looking for ways to measure cultural empathy in order to develop an early warning system to prevent genocide.

ONE OF THE FIRST meetings I went to was "Long-Term Effects of Survival." There was a group of about thirty people, most in their fifties and sixties. It soon became clear that nearly all of them were Jewish survivors of Nazi concentration camps. As this information sank in, my mind began to race. What right did I have to be there? I had not shared their suffering. Was I merely a spectator, satisfying my curiosity? I felt afraid. What if they found out I wasn't Jewish? The only other non-Jews in the room were two Dutch women who had hidden Jews during World War II. Would the survivors identify me with those who had perpetrated the holocaust? Would they turn their anger against me?

Defensively my mind began churning out evidence to show that I'd had nothing to do with the holocaust. I hadn't been there. I was born in 1941 in the United States. Even though my features might appear Aryan, I was not German. Anyway, *I* wouldn't do anything like that.

On the other hand, I found myself wondering what I would have done as a gentile in Nazi Germany. Would I have been immune to the denial, passivity, and disengagement that allowed so many to collaborate in or acquiesce to holocaust? The fear of being part of something fundamentally awful swept over me.

On the second day of the conference I presented a paper on how to talk with children about nuclear war. To my alarm, most of the twenty people attending my talk walked out in the middle. What had I done wrong? Had I somehow offended the holocaust survivors? I was crushed.

Several days later a man from Los Angeles addressed a group of seventy-five people, most of them survivors. "When we saw the Nazis gaining power," he asked, "why didn't we do anything? We knew it was coming. Why didn't we fight?" This is a question that plagues many survivors, and they began to discuss it.

I listened eagerly, for this was above all what I had come for. My assumption was that those who had survived, who knew the costs of denial and passivity, must have thought deeply about what they might have done. Surely the ideas they had developed would be crucial to preventing nuclear holocaust. But as I listened, I heard few ideas and no answers.

The more they talked, the more I felt called to ask my question directly. Finally I stood up, shaking, and spoke from the back row: "I know exactly how you feel. I see a holocaust coming. You say you didn't know where to go, where to hide. The same is true for me. You say it was overwhelming and you didn't believe what you saw. I feel that way now. I may be standing where you were standing in 1939 or 1940." People around me started to cry. "I don't know what to do," I continued. "I've come here to ask you for guidance about how to live in this period and how to prevent a holocaust." When I sat down, the room was absolutely quiet. I knew I had been heard.

Many survivors came up afterward to talk about powerlessness and to empathize with me. Some felt as I did, that a global nuclear holocaust was increasingly likely. And I came to understand why some survivors had walked out during my presentation a few days earlier: they feared they didn't have the strength to face the warnings of another holocaust.

WHILE WE INSIDE THE HILTON were talking about past and future wars, the sound of helicopters overhead reminded us that there was a war going on less than a hundred miles away. Israeli troops were occupying southern Lebanon.

To try to understand the conflicts behind this war better, I resumed my American Willing to Listen project after the conference. In Ramallah, on the West Bank, I sat on the steps of a building at Birzit University and talked with three Palestinian college women. We exchanged jail experiences. They had all been in jail a few times. Once, Israeli soldiers had rounded them up because they were standing near a wall on which an anti-Israeli slogan had been painted. But they didn't have much to say to me about the war in Lebanon.

Then I met a very friendly Palestinian professor of thirty-five or forty. "What is it like for you, knowing what's going on in Lebanon?" I asked. "I have to keep that wall closed," he replied. The war was too painful for him to talk about. When asked why the Palestinian Liberation Organization couldn't recognize Israel, he said that after much discussion in the PLO meetings he'd attended, there was a consensus emerging that it was time to do so.

In Tel Aviv I asked a restaurant owner how the war was affecting him. He was upset because he couldn't serve moussaka, the house specialty, anymore. His moussaka cook had gone off to the war, and all his customers were complaining.

I talked with a twenty-five-year-old woman in the Israeli army. Her regiment had been sent to break up an Israeli peace demonstration in the West Bank. They went in swinging clubs, and the demonstrators fled. Some Israeli Jews had hidden under the counter in a fabric shop run by Palestinians. This woman soldier said the war was driving a wedge between Israeli Jews.

I also followed the war through the local news media, reading the *Jerusalem Post* cover to cover every day and going regularly to the Palestinian News Service to pick up press releases. A woman at the News Service suggested that I go see the war first-hand. She told me I could get press credentials and go into Lebanon in an Israeli Defense Force press car.

I dismissed the idea out of hand. But soon a French journalist asked me to go with him into Lebanon and take photos to accompany his article. It seemed as though opportunity was knocking a second time, urging me to take in this information. Though still strongly resistant to the idea, I began to wonder: How credible is a peace activist who is unwilling to see what she is working against? Why not look directly at the pain rather than working only in the moral abstract?

For years I had been confused by the complexities of the Middle East conflict. Now that I was there, the situation seemed even harder to comprehend. Listening to Israeli Jews and to Palestinian Arabs, I had learned a lot. But deep down I still failed to understand why members of these two groups were hurting each other. I feared that seeing the war would deepen my confusion. And I suspected my own motives. Would I be a voyeur? Was it drama I was seeking? And what if I got caught in the crossfire? I could be killed!

I was afraid, too, that I would see something that would so outrage me that I would try to stop it. I imagined a soldier stopped in a jeep ahead of me shooting helpless people. I might start shouting and try to take the soldier's gun away. I was also afraid I might *not* try to interrupt the war.

AT THE BORDER we signed a release agreeing not to hold the Israeli government responsible if we happened to get killed. That was the first absurdity. The noise of helicopters and gunfire in the distance was ominous. I had to keep reminding myself that this was not a war movie. We climbed aboard an Israeli Defense Force jeep flying a white flag, and drove into Lebanon. Our driver was an IDF press attaché; my fellow passengers were the French journalist and a reporter for a European news service. There was no roof on the jeep, and I thought: What will I do if a hand grenade comes flying in? I'll throw it out. If someone starts shooting at us, I guess I can hide down by the door . . .

It was the first day of the first ceasefire (though there was still shooting going on), and Israeli troops had advanced to within ten miles of Beirut. We drove through the towns of Tyre and Sidon, which had been devastated. Buildings had gaping holes, streets were filled with rubble, walls were riddled with gunshot nicks. In some villages we saw no people at all. Had they been killed, were they hiding, or had they taken flight? In other towns we saw people standing or squatting despondently, talking to each other, shaking their heads. Some gestured wildly. A few times people shouted at us in English, demanding that we press people share with the world what had been done to them. One woman yelled: "You tell them that they bomb schools!"

I felt for the people whose homes and businesses had been shot up and destroyed. Now, instead of making improvements, they would have to rebuild from scratch. The work of whole generations of builders was squandered.

I was surprised to see soldiers resting, eating little crackers. I had never pictured a war zone as a place where soldiers could have cracker breaks.

As we drove along, our guide would point to a destroyed building and explain, "We found rifles here," or "This was a PLO headquarters." We came upon a school for mentally retarded children that had been bombed to ruins. Children walked around aimlessly, confusion on their faces. Many had been badly hurt and were bandaged up. A boy about twelve years old wailed unceasingly as he clung to a tree, his body rocking back and forth. Our guide said he didn't know anything about this bombing. We were outraged, and grew silent as we took in the scene.

We stopped at a civilian hospital, where I saw people of all ages who were horribly hurt. A woman came up to talk to me, speaking rapidly in Arabic, with her face close to mine. As our guide translated, I learned that her home had been bombed, one of her children had been killed and another had been injured. She was hysterical. Helpless to do anything, I felt sorrow in every muscle of my body. I put my arm on her shoulder and said, "I'm sorry, I'm so very sorry."

Once, as our group of four stood on a little rise, a shell exploded fifty yards away—where we had just driven. Could they be shooting at us? I started to tremble and felt wetness trickling down my legs. Our guide hurried us off. In that moment, as we rushed into the jeep and bounced away, I knew I never wanted war to happen to me again, I never wanted it to happen to my friends and family, and I never wanted it to happen to people who were not yet my friends.

BACK IN ISRAEL, I kept thinking about what I'd seen, re-running it in my mind—the rubble, the blank faces, the people screaming in the hospital. One day of seeing the terror had filled me with sadness, confusion, and fear. How do people survive through war day after day? For several nights, I couldn't sleep.

I got angrier and angrier. I was angry that somebody had ordered this misery to happen, had deliberately decided on it. I was angry that the women, the mentally-retarded children, and the old people were suffering so. I was angry at the Israelis for starting the war; I was angry at the PLO for storing all the weapons which had served as the Israelis' pretext for invasion. I was angry that this had been going on for thirty years. I was angry because neither side had just stopped!

I made a return visit to Birzit University in Ramallah, feeling surprisingly at home as I chatted with Palestinian students and their architecture professor. I was impressed with the informality between them—they talked and joked as friends. Then we heard that Israeli troops had surrounded the campus and were not letting anyone come or go. This had happened before; it was a form of harassment the students and faculty had learned to endure. They began to prepare for a protracted stay, rationing food from the cafeteria and holding meetings. Students and faculty considered resisting the troops in honor of their "fallen allies in Lebanon," but decided instead to take a wait-and-see posture. I was able to leave the university in a reporter's car and never learned how much longer the siege continued.

I went to Tel Aviv the next day to see Shlomo, a man I had met while attending the holocaust conference. He was in the electronics business and, like many other middle-aged Israeli men, was also a reserve officer in the army. As we walked along the Mediterranean, I poured out my anger and deep confusion about the war. Shlomo was a caring, intelligent person; he listened and shared his own ambivalent feelings. Though he felt drawn to fellow Israelis who were protesting the war, he was still ready to serve if called up by the military. Shlomo also told me about the sufferings of Israeli people at the hands of the Palestinians—the people killed in terrorist bombings of schoolbuses, airports, kibbutzes.

At the end of our conversation I felt only more confused. I was sure of just one thing: there was too much suffering in that region. Shaken, I left Israel the next day.

On the plane, images from my trip came to mind: holocaust survivors, war victims, students and teachers at Birzit, my friend Shlomo. The farther I got from the Middle East, the more clearly I could see that both sides in the conflict were absolutely right, correct in every detail. Both had just causes, and each had been wronged by the other. People on both sides had told me of atrocities committed by the other; each side blamed the other for starting it, and no one seemed to know where it would end. Both sides were absolutely right—except that they were killing each other. What does a responsible person do in such a situation?

UPON MY RETURN HOME, friends asked me to tell them about my trip. Usually I love to tell stories, but the experience of touching the war was something I did not want to share. And it has not gotten much easier with time.

I don't want to tell you about the faces of the people I saw in Lebanon. I don't even want to remember. The pain that I glimpsed—pain that was deliberately caused by policy and design—is so obscene that my civilized mind censors it for you. Perhaps that censorship angers you. It angers me too. I am furious that some people can create pain so horrible that it violates the human spirit to remember.

It does not surprise me that soldiers do not want to tell their families and friends about their war experiences. I can begin to understand why some of those who live with the memory of war never recover from it. And I have a better sense of how difficult it must be for Vietnam veterans to try to resume their normal lives after participating in such a horrible, connection-shattering event as war.

What angers me most about war is what it does to our confidence in our fellow beings. War is the ultimate succumbing, the final failure of resolve to make things work out well for everyone involved.

As I feared, seeing war has shaken my optimism and customary happiness. I've begun to wonder why we in the United States seem so happy and optimistic. Is part of the reason that there have been no wars on our land in the last century? We do not carry memories of disruption in the flow of human affairs, so we can obsess about the latest fashions, the top-ranked football teams, and other frivolities. I do not wonder that people from the Middle East cling so tenaciously to life.

Although I had seen only one day of a relatively small conventional war, it was several months before I stopped waking up at night sweating with fear, before the memories stopped playing like a continuous movie in the back of my mind, before I could return to the security of being an American woman who isn't supposed to have to think about such things.

It was the Nazi holocaust that first convinced me that human beings—former sweet babies, innocent schoolchildren, loving parents, people who worked hard for a living—could perpetrate horrors against other human beings, who were also former sweet babies, innocent schoolchildren, loving family members. Part of me wants to say, "We would never do anything like that. Americans aren't like that." But no society is free of shame. We Americans must face our Ku Klux Klan, the slaughter of our native peoples, the Dresden firebombing, the atomic bombings of Hiroshima and Nagasaki, the internment of our Japanese citizens during World War II, the Vietnam War, the My Lai massacre, and our preparations for all-out nuclear war. We are not immune from contemplating, planning, and carrying out unspeakable horrors.

Human beings have the ability to run amok. The Nazi holocaust didn't happen only to Europeans. The war in Lebanon isn't happening only to the people in the Middle East. These things happen to our species. That's us.

9 | *How Can I Keep from Laughing?*

ABOUT TEN YEARS AGO I realized that the way I was reading the newspaper wasn't working. I really wanted to know what was going on in the world, but all the stories about horrors and disasters only left me feeling numb and helpless. Watching the news on TV was an even more passive, disempowering experience. It almost seemed as though the newspaper publishers and TV broadcasters were programming us to look to the ads for relief from their news, to buoy up the consumer world. "The world may be falling apart, but you can fix yourself up at Macy's."

I started experimenting with less passive ways of absorbing the news. I talked back to the television set, ripped up the newspaper,

119

and finally began to develop a comedy act about the news. Comedy seemed a natural medium for me. I had grown up in a pre-TV family; we spent many nights laughing together at the absurdities of life and at each other's funniness. I have always enjoyed telling stories and laughing.

So I got up on stage at a coffeehouse in San Francisco and began to explore current events with the audience. I read choice items from the *San Francisco Chronicle*, personalizing the news.

One of my big shows, planned well in advance, occurred a few days after the People's Temple mass suicide in Guyana. I didn't know how I could do the show with my heart so heavy and my mind so confused about the tragedy. So I mixed a little reality in with the comedy, and people seemed relieved to have that balance. I started wondering whether there could be a social form, a niche in our community life, called "realedy"— neither comedy nor tragedy but a lively mix of the two. I envisioned a forum where we could talk about our lives, share the absurdities we saw around us. Realedy would serve as a vehicle to help us come out of the closet with what was really happening in our world and in our hearts.

THE IDEA OF DOING a ventriloquist act with the American flag occurred to me one day while I was preparing for a show. I had already experimented with standing the flag next to me onstage; I would nudge it and talk to it as I read the newspaper. Now I wanted it to have a voice of its own. Since I wasn't a ventriloquist, I asked my good friend Charlie Varon to play the voice of the flag. I bought a small flag and sewed an extra layer of cloth on the back of the stars. I would put my hand inside and move the flag's "mouth" while Charlie spoke his lines offstage.

The character we began to develop was a crotchety guy with a lot of problems. Memory problems (he couldn't remember whether the mission to rescue U.S. hostages from Iran had succeeded or failed), hearing problems (he heard "erection" for "election"), ego problems (he worried that the Soviet Union had bigger missiles than he did). He was not a malevolent guy, not inherently evil. But he did make mistakes and often failed to comprehend the pain his mistakes caused. He was upset that upstart countries like Iran were giving him a hard time, confounded that the rest of the world wouldn't always cooperate with his plans. When it came right down to it, he wasn't afraid to push to get his way.

Then Charlie and I got an idea for a sketch that had little to do with politics: an interview with Dr. Earlina Johnson, a woman who had invented a new kind of sex, called transformational sex. I learned how little I knew about acting as I tried to overcome embarrassment and get beyond the limits of my own personality. I had to get absolutely carried away as I described the joys of "new sex" and simulated a wild orgasm. We went to a couple of local comedy clubs and tried the sketch out, with marginal success.

Meanwhile, my explorations with the nuclear study group had begun to show me the comic possibilities tied up in the nuclear threat. After I had done some research into the government's plans for civil defense, I called up the regional office of the Federal Emergency Management Agency.

"I have just a few questions after reading all your literature," I said. "How can you get radiation out of the air that's coming into your fallout shelter?"

"We don't know," came the reply. "The Congress cut that research out of the budget."

"Well, what about the soil? After a nuclear war, won't the soil be so radioactive that the food produced on it would be hazardous?"

"That's another area the government hasn't funded. Sorry."

I discovered the sheer power of laughing in the face of the bomb at our nuclear study group's weekend retreat. After being overwhelmed by despair, we had inexplicably started laughing. And the laughter had released a tremendous amount of energy. After that experience I told Charlie, "We've got to start doing nuclear comedy." I could see that comedy would be needed to help fight the sadness and despair that people faced as they grappled with the nuclear threat. It would be a ministry to hold up the absurdity of the situation without belittling the problems posed by the bomb. Charlie was a little surprised at my idea, but a few days later brought over a short story he had secretly written a year or two before, called "Proliferation." It was about a bank vice-president who wins a friend's nuclear bomb in a poker game, puts it in a safety deposit box, and learns to make love to it. So we made an intuitive leap and started calling ourselves "nuclear comedians."

MY DAD USED TO TELL US that during the Depression, some people became more decent, generous, and honest. Others became more suspicious, greedy, and hateful. He said he hoped that, if we faced that kind of stressful situation, we would act decently.

How can we find ways to be decent in the face of the nuclear terror? When I am terrified, I tend to lose clarity, take rash or self-serving action, or do nothing at all. But what happens when a whole population gets scared? When an entire society is filled with the fear of a war, or worse yet a nuclear war? All that fear, all the crazy things that occur to people, all the panic and paralysis, all the grasping for control and the egotistical efforts to be heroic—these responses scare me.

During the Black Plague, another period of terror, the social order dissolved into ugliness and hysteria. In our own time, People's Temple minister Jim Jones repeatedly used the fear of nuclear holocaust to manipulate his followers into extreme acts.

As a climate of crisis and hysteria builds, we lose confidence in ourselves and each other. We have trouble thinking flexibly and moving calmly and rationally toward solutions to our massive problems.

I thought nuclear comedy could provide one small part of the antidote to that hysteria. Seeing the absurdity of the nuclear situation might help people release some of their fear and gain a little perspective. It might free some of the creativity and energy bound up in the fear. And, if done in a friendly social setting, nuclear comedy might build people's sense of confidence and connectedness.

ONE OF THE FIRST nuclear comedy sketches we developed was called "What About the Russians?" Charlie plays an on-the-street radio interviewer who accosts passerby Patricia May Nicholson with the question: "What should we do about the Russians?" Patricia May responds: "Oh, you'll have to ask my husband that question." The more insistent the interviewer becomes, trying to whip her into an anti-Soviet frenzy, the kinder and more genteel Patricia May becomes. Finally, when asked to imagine what she'd do if the Russians landed in her home town, she says: "Have they had dinner? If they like

American food, we could have them up to the church for supper. After all, they've come all this way."

Another early routine was an interview with a hopelessly inept minor-league baseball pitcher named Dusty Molloy. Dusty has been in a slump for a while; his record is three wins and sixteen losses. Dusty is unperturbed by his own mediocrity—he has a casual "win some, lose some" attitude. But there is a problem with the team's front office. They make unrealistic promises to the fans—promises of shutout games, no-hit games, pennant seasons. Meanwhile, Dusty is out on the mound trying his level best just to find home plate.

It turns out that in the off-season Dusty has another job: he works at a nuclear power plant. "Nuclear power is just like baseball," Dusty remarks. "You have a front office making all kinds of ridiculous promises to the fans: no leaks, no spills, no plant shutdowns. They're promising the fans perfection." But, as Dusty casually explains, "perfection just isn't human nature."

Charlie and I owe our friendship to the Diablo Canyon nuclear power plant near San Luis Obispo, California, where we both participated in a civil disobedience action in 1978. As the plant's design troubles worsened in 1981, we found ourselves laughing more and more about nuclear power.

Pacific Gas and Electric had decided to build the Diablo Canyon plant in the late 1960s, when nuclear power plants were in vogue. Then they found that an earthquake fault ran within a few miles of the plant—and they tried to squelch the information. That was the beginning of a comedy of errors. The Nuclear Regulatory Commission ordered PG & E to install safety brackets to protect against earthquakes, but the brackets were installed backwards. Every time the plant was about to be licensed, another flaw or cover-up would be revealed. How could we keep from laughing? We remembered Dusty's words about perfection and human nature, and we created a "corporate sympathy" greeting card for PG & E.

One day Charlie arrived for rehearsal just as Alex, a realtor friend of mine, was leaving. Charlie and I tried to interest Alex in the nuclear issue. He didn't seem responsive, so we began to tell him what nuclear war would do to the real estate market. Thus our "Realtors for Social Responsibility" sketch was born. I play RSR founder Hermione Pledge; Charlie is again an earnest interviewer.

"Mrs. Pledge, what is the basic concern of your group?"

"Nuclear war would take property off the market. A nuclear explosion sucks up pieces of real estate into a mushroom cloud. That's what a mushroom cloud is! It's pieces of property that have been sucked up and made radioactive; then they fall down on *other* pieces of property—what you might call 'hot property'. And that's not to mention that in the same mushroom cloud, neighborhoods would mix!"

We had such fun inventing sketches. Some nights the material came rolling off our hearts like an avalanche. We screamed with delight at each new idea. After rehearsal, we would go out for ice cream with our friend Myra, who had become the producer and censor of our comedy show. We'd get our ice cream, sit in the car, and perform the evening's new material for Myra. Occasionally she would shake her head and say, "Well, I don't know," and we would know that we had gone past the bounds of good taste and common decency. To be a comedian, one has to suspend certain limits on sensibility which normal society uses to keep itself civilized. Myra has always played that discretionary role for us and saved us from our most disgusting selves.

OUR FRIEND Jim Rosenau suggested that we develop a full show and perform it at a friend's house. So we invited all our friends to a Sunday night show at Myra's mother's house, and they laughed enough to encourage us but not so much as to delude us into thinking we were very good comedians yet. Charlie had had some dramatic training in college but I had taken only one drama class in high school and one at summer camp when I was twelve years old. Acting wasn't fun for me. Communicating was. The transaction with the audience—watching them listen and reflect—was the thrill. And applause was a real torture. We performed together four years before I could ever enjoy the applause. I think I must be a shy person trapped in the body of an extrovert.

We continued performing in San Francisco, trying out our sketches for audiences at nuclear freeze petition parties. And then we set out on two tours in February of 1982: one to the East Coast and one to Colorado. Everywhere we went there were small but enthusiastic audiences. After the shows, people often came up to thank us for helping them laugh at the nuclear threat. We balanced our comedy shows with a few minutes of serious talking from the stage, and with workshops on the psychological toll of the arms race. We called the program "Living and Laughing in the Nuclear Age."

Our Colorado tour organizer, Carol Rothman, showed us a piece of "indigenous nuclear comedy": a government booklet entitled "Crisis Relocation: Guidance for Residents of the Denver Metropolitan Area." It was all about leaving the "risk area" and relocating to an outlying "host area" in the event of a threatened nuclear attack. At one show at a nightclub in Denver, we tried out some of the "material" that had been written by the government:

"Before you leave home, close all curtains and drapes and turn all home heating and appliance thermostats to lowest setting . . . Be advised that your pet may be placed in a temporary pet shelter . . . You are NOT encouraged to take firearms to the Host Area . . . What to take with you. Prepare to take those things that you would take on a two week vacation trip, plus . . ." Then there is a checklist that includes such items as work gloves, work clothes, shovels, axes, picks—it's going to be a hell of a vacation!—as well as deeds, insurance policies, stocks and bonds.

And then—the government is so thoughtful—the booklet suggests bringing "extra underclothing." I guess they figure we'll see the nuclear explosion and just shit in our pants.

The Denver audience was howling at all this, but they absolutely exploded when we read: "What to expect on the road: Traffic will probably be heavy . . ." We've kept the Denver "Crisis Relocation" pamphlet in the show; it's one of our funniest sketches. We can't write material as good as that.

THERE WAS ANOTHER SHOW on that tour that I'll never forget. Looking out at a packed auditorium at the University of Colorado in Boulder, I saw several people laughing with their hands clasped around their heads. It was as if little comedy bombs were going off inside and they were trying to hold their heads together. At another show, from her vantage point at the light and sound controls, Myra saw a woman laughing so hard that other members of the audience kept looking to see if she was okay.

I often feel comedy bombs going off inside me when we generate material. One afternoon Charlie and I were working on our sketch about Colonel Curtis Catapult, a twenty-one-year veteran of the

U.S. Airborne who was recently traded to the Soviet Army. We had already established his fondness for Russian vodka and his professionalism—being traded didn't affect his love for "the game." But the sketch hadn't taken off. Then it happened. Colonel Catapult started spinning out a plan to retrofit Soviet nuclear missiles with motorcycle seats, handlebars, and maps with little arrows, so his Airborners could ride them down. Why sit on the sidelines in a nuclear war? Naturally, the boys in the Soviet Airborne had never seen the United States, and they wanted to, and a nuclear war might be their only chance. So Colonel Catapult decided to circle some tourist spots on the maps, like the Empire State Building and the Golden Gate Bridge, so the boys could enjoy some sightseeing before continuing on to their targets.

Sometimes I feel as though there are two realities separated by a curtain. One reality is our daily lives; we see people scurrying around, doing their work, living their lives. But every now and then we peek out from behind the curtain, and see a second reality: the world as a whole, poised on the brink of several disasters at once, our planet befouled, starvation, oppression, war, invasion, fifty thousand nuclear weapons . . . "Hey, there is a world out there, and the situation is really absurd! Oh my heavens, is this *us*? How embarrassing!" The two realities collide for a moment: I feel like a hostage on a planet of fundamentally crazy people, and I suspect I may be one of them.

Then I recoil for a while at the insanity of it all, and close the curtain. A wave of sadness, anger, or fear passes through me. Then something starts to go off inside me again. I peek through the curtain once more, and through the terror and insanity, a roar from deep inside comes up and out. It is a cosmic roar, a roar of survival, a burst of true energy that relieves just enough of my suffering to unleash the fury to heal and work even harder.

I felt energized for about two weeks after we created our "Wrath of God" sketch. Gabriel brings God the news that the human beings down on the planet Earth have just started a global thermonuclear war. At first, God can't believe it; then he turns angry. "If I told them once, I told them a million times: 'Don't leave it all up to me!' They said, 'God won't let a nuclear war happen.' Those infantile jerks! They probably thought nuclear war would bring on Armageddon and they'd get a free trip up to heaven. Well, they've got something else coming. Close the gates, Gabriel! No one else gets in! Anyone who would let this happen—let them stay down there on earth and rot!"

We performed "The Wrath of God" as part of a lecture we gave to a religion class at a college in northwestern Iowa. After the sketch, a thoughtful young woman asked us if we didn't think God was a forgiving god. Wouldn't He forgive us if we had a nuclear war?

I've thought a lot about that question since then. I imagine arriving in heaven, waiting in a long line with all the other creatures, and finally getting to the Judge. He looks at me.

"Were you party to this mess, Frances Peavey?"

"Yes, sir."

"What do you have to say for yourself?"

"Well, God, it kind of got away from us. Before we knew it, we had a big stockpile and a lot of industrial and psychological investment in continuing the effort. And, well, we didn't seem to know how to turn around once we had come so far. That's the truth. We didn't do it on purpose."

God just sits there, overwhelmed by sadness, thinking of all the lilies of the field and the sparrows destroyed in the holocaust.

"And what part did *you* play?" He asks me.

"Well, God, I paid taxes for the weapons for a while, and I thought the bombs weren't so bad. And what else? Well, I was just a small part of the whole thing."

Somehow it sounds a little foolish to ask forgiveness at that point.

I OFTEN TELL AUDIENCES about my dawning realization that the U.S. and Soviet governments are out to kill me. They are building more and more nuclear weapons, developing first-strike weapons, stationing them all over the world—and the result of all this is going to be *my* death. And as if that isn't bad enough, the U.S. government wants me to pay them for this—through federal income taxes. That seems like a cost overrun of giant proportions. If I wanted to commit suicide, I could buy a gun for $45 and shoot myself, or I could jump off the Golden Gate Bridge for free.

Over the years, I've been putting a lot of time and energy into staying alive. I've been buckling my seatbelt, avoiding foods that contain hazardous additives, brushing my teeth so they'd last for the rest of my life. And all of that just doesn't seem consistent with paying for nuclear weapons. So I've stopped paying federal taxes. Now I can brush my teeth with a clear conscience.

The decision to stop paying taxes wasn't really a strategical or political act. It wasn't because I thought it was "the right thing to do." It was because I could no longer invest any of the fruits of my life in those weapons. Maybe it was because my father was an insurance man who taught me to act responsibly in the present so as not to live in regret in the future. Preventing nuclear war is just like trying to protect my house from fire: I'm careful about the wiring in my home, and keep fire extinguishers in the logical places, so that if the house burns down at least I'll know I did everything I could have done.

The thought has occurred to me that someday, somewhere, I might look up and see the mushroom cloud. That day, in those last few moments, I want to have as few regrets as possible. I don't want to hate myself for my part in the madness. It was as an investment in my own mental health at that potential moment in time that I decided to stop paying taxes.

TRAVELING WITH OUR COMEDY SHOW, talking with people all over, we have learned a lot about the price we are paying for nuclear weapons and the defense policy East and West seem wedded to.

In the spring of 1983, we toured up and down Great Britain, performing in alternative "fringe" theatres. The parliamentary election campaign was in full swing. Nuclear policy was a key issue, with the Labour Party challenging the conservative Thatcher government's position and arguing for unilateral British nuclear disarmament.

We were surprised and pleased that our British audiences liked nuclear comedy so much. The American flag sketch was a real hit, especially the flag's extemporaneous answering of questions from the audience.

The country whose empire once dominated the world now seems to be occupied by the United States. Britain, a country no larger than northern California, houses more than one hundred U.S. military bases, and the U.S. nuclear weapons stationed there are under American control. "I'm having some troubles with Great Britain," the flag said. "We just can't figure out which of us is the empire and which is the colony."

We took our show to Greenham Common, the U.S. airbase where cruise missiles were to be (and have since been) installed, and the site of some of the most determined work against deployment—including a permanent women's peace camp. Rather a strange collection of women were gathered there. There were grandmothers, housewives who had left home to stop the arms race and whose kids visited them on weekends, an infant who had been born at the peace camp, and one very "punk" woman who wore safety pins poked through skin flaps in the bridge of her nose, her ears, and between her fingers. She must have been wearing twenty safety pins in places I could see, and I wondered about the places I couldn't. Looking at her made my teeth vibrate and hurt, so I had a lot of trouble looking very long. Later, the other women told me stories about her work which allowed me to see that there was more to her than the safety pins.

We had somehow forgotten to bring our props with us to the peace camp, and several women set about finding some hats which might be appropriate for our characters. We cut out a red star for Colonel Catapult's hat, and someone stuck it on a plastic policeman's hat with Marmite, a particularly viscous food spread which the British seem to put on everything they eat. They suggested that we perform as close to the gate as possible, because the American guards get bored and might appreciate a comedy break. Word went out that a comedy team from America was doing a show at the main gate, and women from several campsites gathered there, squatting against the fence. It began to drizzle. Military cars and trucks, some with U.S. license plates, whizzed in and out of the gate. I felt like Bob Hope, entertaining the warriors, giving them a break from their weary task.

Several days later, at the U.S. Air Force base at Upper Heyford, we performed for some of the peace activists who were blockading the base. Our "stage" was a one-foot-wide strip between two white lines on the motorway pavement. Behind us, a row of British police officers and passing cars; in front, a bulging crowd of protesters, more police, and two military men peering out from behind the fence. As we did our "Colonel Catapult" sketch, the enthusiastic crowd grew larger, overflowing onto the road. The police officers got so involved in the show that they let the crowd grow until there was a traffic jam.

ANOTHER TOUR TOOK US to the Deep West—Nevada, Utah, Colorado, Wyoming, Montana, and my home state of Idaho. An hour out of Las Vegas our rented car broke down and a stranger came to our aid. He was a retired Marine who had transported nuclear weapons around the country. An appropriate start to our tour, we thought. While we waited for our replacement car, we chatted awhile.

Bob told us that his brother, who had served in the army, had been exposed to radiation during an aboveground weapons test at the Nevada Test Site in the fifties, and later died of cancer. As for nuclear war, Bob said, "Dead's dead." Still, he expected that a nuclear war would be Armageddon and counted himself among the faithful who'd be saved. He was so tedious on this point that later Charlie referred to him as "Bobageddon."

A few days later, we found ourselves standing where Bob's brother had stood some thirty years before. People from all over had come to a peace vigil at the Nevada Test Site. Busloads of workers drove past us. Some workers waved. I kept wondering how they felt about their work, and what its impact was on their health and the quality of their lives.

And I remembered the atomic veterans I'd met in other parts of the country who had been exposed during weapons tests. They had been told to place their hands over their eyes when the bomb exploded, but the light from the blast was so intense that they had seen the bones in their hands, even with their eyes closed. One ex-soldier remembered having the strong conviction, upon seeing the bomb go off, that there was no god. God would not bestow such a horrible power on man.

Our next stop was southwest Utah, an area downwind of the Test Site. The jump in the cancer rate there has been linked to the radiation released by atmospheric tests during the fifties. Though aboveground testing has been banned, accidental leaks from underground tests are not infrequent—one occurred a few days before we arrived.

People we met were angry and felt betrayed by their government— which had told them the fallout they saw on their land and in the air was safe. Now they felt their loyalty and patriotism had been used against them. They had clear evidence of the rottenness issuing forth from the nuclear madness; they were painfully reminded of it every day. An older man named Ike had lost his wife to cancer and carried his bitterness heavily. He told us he hadn't laughed since his wife had died, and didn't think he could. But when he saw some of our sketches, he laughed in spite of himself.

We returned to Boulder, one of the great nuclear comedy towns in the country, to participate in the Conference on World Affairs. There we met Mira Petrovskaya, a woman who works with the Soviet bureau that studies the United States and Canada. She got to see some of our sketches, including "Colonel Catapult" and "What Should We Do About the Russians?" She enjoyed the idea of nuclear comedy and told us she didn't know of any nuclear comedians in the Soviet Union. We all became concerned that the Soviets had fallen behind in the nuclear comedy race.

In Wyoming and Montana, we met activists working against the deployment of MX missiles, and in Great Falls, Montana, we performed our "Wrath of God" sketch at an Easter Day service and rally at the Malmstrom Air Force Base, which controls hundreds of Minuteman missiles. Driving back from the rally, we saw a strange, fenced-in circular area by the side of the highway. A friend from Helena who was riding with us told us it was one of the many Minuteman silos that dot Montana.

I SHUDDER EVERY TIME I see another strand of the nuclear web we human beings are weaving. Denial becomes more difficult as we travel the "nuclear circuit," as we stand at Malmstrom Air Force Base, at the Nevada Test Site, at Greenham Common, as we meet atomic veterans, downwind victims, uranium miners. But hopelessness also becomes more difficult: everywhere we travel, even in small towns like Sheridan, Wyoming, and Storm Lake, Iowa, we meet people working with determination to prevent nuclear war and reclaim the future. My own home town of Twin Falls now has an active peace group.

And there are other signs of hope: on our second tour to the Pacific Northwest, we returned to Vancouver, British Columbia, and Bellingham, Washington. In the year since we'd first performed there, both cities had declared themselves nuclear-free zones.

Outside Madison, Wisconsin (itself a nuclear-free zone), Charlie and I toured the American Breeders Service plant, the world's largest producer, or rather collector, of bull semen. Through scientific breeding and artificial insemination, dairy cattle in the United States now produce much more milk per capita than they used to. And, we found out, the Soviet Union recently purchased millions of dollars of bull semen from ABS to improve Soviet dairy cattle. This means that there are now hundreds of thousands of Soviet-American cows running around the USSR. Would we have the heart to bomb cattle that are part of our family?

EVERY DAY I AM BARRAGED with grim news about people violating the life on this planet: wars, murders, suicides, rapes, ecological disasters. And, in my brief snatch of time on this beautiful planet, I have to contemplate the possibility that all this beauty could end in a puff of radioactivity.

Yes, the danger is real, and we may not get through it. But instead of cowering in the face of doom, I choose to face the mushroom cloud and roar with laughter. That laughter slices into the nuclear silence and penetrates even my own numbness.

I have no commitment to change as a panacea. In fact the real goal is continuity, which is a kind of stability. The splendid evolutionary paradox is that continuity requires constant sensitive readjustment—not only change but precise change.

Stewart Brand

10 |*The Power of Context*

AFTER A MONTH ON THE JOB as a teacher at Roosevelt Junior High School, I was given a whistle by the principal. Between classes, I would leave my classroom and go to a yellow circle painted on the floor of the hall. I was expected to stand on the circle, blow my whistle, and yell at the students. In retrospect I'm embarrassed that I, a mature adult, participated in something so silly. But that activity was part of the generally accepted behavior, and I was among those who accepted it.

Had I stopped to think about it, I might have realized that such authoritarian behavior not only increased the disorder in the hallway; it was also contrary to my personal values and educational philosophy. Instead, I acted in accordance with the expectations of my social context.

Each of us is under constant pressure to conform to social norms; we get signals from people around us about which ideas, activities, and changes are appropriate to consider and which are not. It is our social context that directs our attention and gives us cues for our thinking, behavior, and beliefs.

Growing up in Idaho, I was struck by the contradiction between the good, Christian values of the rancher friends of my family, and the fact that they provided poor housing for their Mexican fieldworkers. Since then, I have come to understand some of the social dynamics behind this contradiction. The ranchers were accountable to a narrow context, made up of ranchers and other white landowners. Barriers of race, class, and culture kept Mexican fieldworkers from being a powerful force in this social context. The social relationships and the economic relationships rested on each other.

There remained a conflict for the ranchers, between their Christian values (wanting to do right by their workers) and their perceived self-interest (wanting to increase their own material well-being). But the ranchers' context did not encourage them to resolve the conflict in favor of their best wishes for their workers. Even when profits were high, it was socially acceptable to continue allowing the fieldworkers to live in shacks. The work camp had been built many years before, and the issue was considered closed.

Contextual assumptions are our unconscious filtering system, defining the limits of what we consider possible. Bees have a similar perceptual filter, but in their case it is a physical one. Bees' eyes are composed of thousands of hexagonal facets; they see the world in hexagons. Is it a coincidence that they build each cell of their hives in the shape of a hexagon? For human beings, our contextual and cultural assumptions determine the shape of what we see and what we create. It's difficult to recognize these assumptions, let alone question them. I've come to believe that even those among us who are more independent-minded can question only about 30 percent of our contextual assumptions.

Moving into a new context, even temporarily, can shift our assumptions and behavior. For example, in my neighborhood grocery store in San Francisco, it was almost natural for my grandmother to hug my black friend Deputy. After all, I was the person there who cared most about the way she behaved, and she knew I would want her to be friendly. So she adapted herself, at least for the moment, to this new context. My grandmother would have been much less likely to hug him if she had been accompanied by her husband, her daughter, or a friend from her bridge club back home.

The long-term effect of this encounter on my grandmother's feelings about black people was probably minimal. One such experience could not fundamentally challenge the whole set of attitudes and behavior that constitute racism. Unlearning racism requires making strong connections with blacks and, based on those connections, developing a new view of black people—one that contradicts and eventually overrides the old prejudices.

The process of creating Sixth Street Park reshaped the context of the street people there. The expectations and values associated with the park were different from those that had previously prevailed on Sixth Street. The park context discouraged violence; it supported caring, socially-responsible behavior, and encouraged taking pride in one's contributions. Quite often street people responded to these "noble" cues rather than to violent, selfish, or self-destructive ones.

UNDERSTANDING THE POWER OF CONTEXT helps me understand change. It gives me a framework for understanding that when people act in ways that seem inconsistent with their basic humanity, it may not mean they are basically horrible human beings.

Take the example of a young man who is drafted, leaves home, and goes through military training. He is thrust into a setting where the rules are at odds with his previous home-and-school context, where he was taught that killing people is unacceptable behavior. Now, in this new context, he shifts to accommodate the new values and expectations: in a war, he kills.

The idea of context also helps me understand inertia in institutions. Imagine that twelve of us are sitting on the board of directors of a corporation that has for decades been dumping chemical wastes into a river. We have all been presiding over that activity for some time. As individuals in the privacy of our kitchens, we may each have doubts about the morality of the dumping. But when we gather in the boardroom, those personal opinions lose significance. Here we answer to the ideology and expectations of the system, to the accepted practice of the corporation. We find mental devices to override our doubts about polluting: "Well, a different method of disposal would affect our profitability. We can't afford it." "This isn't my specialty." "Probably other people have thought this out."

ON A PERSONAL LEVEL, seeing the power of context has prompted me to examine the context I am accountable to. Like most people, I am generally more comfortable with those who share my culture and values. Consciously or unconsciously, most of us have been raised to love our families and the people most like us, and to distrust people who are different. As a result, our social context tends to be rather homogeneous, our field of concern relatively narrow.

But this narrowness makes certain dangerous conclusions seem appropriate. When Carl Reiner interviewed the 2000-year-old man as played by his comedy partner, Mel Brooks, he asked whether, in the "rocks and caves days," Brooks' cave had an anthem. "Of course," replied Brooks. "It went like this: 'Let 'em all go to hell, except Cave 76!' "

It has seemed important to make conscious efforts to broaden the context I am accountable to. Of these, the most effective have been those which gave me direct, personal experiences with people who are different from me.

You can learn only a limited amount about fish by going to an aquarium. You can see what they look like, how they swim, and how they eat in an alien environment. But you don't learn much about the everyday life of an average fish. For example, you don't learn anything about predators. Of course, a trip to the aquarium is safer than going to the fishes' environment because you don't have to worry about drowning or being attacked by sharks—or even getting wet. The aquarium is a good place to start one's aquatic education, but it's important to understand how that context affects what you learn.

Going *into* the black community was an important element of my black lessons. As a teacher, I got some impressions of my black students' lives. But the information I got was skewed because in the classroom the power was disproportionately mine. The kids were adapting their behavior to the rules of the school context. By going into a situation where their culture was dominant, with someone from their culture as my "guide," I was a little closer to seeing the world from their perspective.

My American Willing to Listen project was also designed to give those I listened to the "homecourt advantage." I can meet Thai people in the United States, but they have of necessity adapted to our society. Going to Thailand, I was the one who had to make the adjustments, who had to forego the security of assuming that my patterns of thinking and understanding, and my value system, were shared by those around me. Naturally, this made me feel vulnerable and often uncomfortable. But the paradox is that by making myself more vulnerable, I gradually come to feel less threatened by differences and more at home in a variety of contexts. The long-term result is a deep sense of security.

Making connections like these makes me feel accountable to people whose lives are very different from my own. When I was teaching counseling, two students made a point of educating me about what the world looked like to gay people and how they experienced oppression. Later, when an anti-gay policy statement was printed in a national newsletter, I felt, out of loyalty to my students, that I had to take a stand against that statement. As a woman, a fat person, and a former child, I know what such injustice feels like from the inside, and I know the value of having allies against that injustice.

Another time, in a gas station, a white customer was complaining to the Chinese attendant about "awful black people." I was just standing there, waiting to pay for my gas. But I had to speak up: "That's not right," I said. "That's prejudice talking. You can't talk about my friends that way."

I can also think of many times when, at the crucial moment, the accountability I felt was not powerful enough to overcome my own shyness and reluctance to take a risk. Afterwards I felt I had betrayed my friends and what I knew. I was left wondering what I could have done that would have been more effective and more true to my relationship to my friends. All too often, I have other opportunities to take such risks.

But this kind of accountability also calls forth more subtle responses. For example, when I'm deciding how to vote, I now find it impossible not to think about the people I've met around the world whose lives are affected by U.S. policy. I can almost sense the Nonaligned Nations delegate from Tonga looking over my shoulder as I make my choices.

ONE OF THE MOST DIFFICULT PARTS of broadening my context has been coming to terms with the pain in the lives of people I have come to care about. Many nights during the International Hotel campaign, I would return to my secure home, where I had four or five times as much living space as the hotel tenants and where I faced no threat of eviction. On the nights I had to teach, I wrestled with the decision to place my personal and family needs above those of the tenants. Even while relaxing or making love, I would find myself thinking of them and their suffering.

After getting to know some of the street people at Sixth Street Park, I experienced the winter differently. Snuggled in my warm bed, I pictured eight or ten men huddled around a fire at the park. On cold, rainy days, I often think about the people on Sixth Street and what I can do to help them.

It has been painful for me to love people who are poor and down-and-out. It has meant I must somehow acknowledge that I can do very little to substantially change their situation. And yet I must help in the ways I can. As I become a more reliable ally of people different from me, I feel less guilt about our relationship. This, in turn, makes it easier for me to make connections with them.

Working with people who have suffered as a result of oppression seems to mean I must prepare myself to be yelled at, or at least distrusted. No matter how hard I try, it seems inevitable that I'll say or do something hurtful to the black or Jewish or disabled person I'm working with.

"You're just like I expected!" they'll yell. Then some horrible anger, some invective against me, my behavior, my people. It feels like an avalanche. I feel as though I may deserve a little shovelful of snow for my error, but instead, a whole mountain of snow, complete with boulders, is dropped on me. Each time, I imagine I won't come out alive. I feel terrible about myself: I must be a horrible, arrogant person, as bad as a slaveowner; I, single-handedly, am holding back a whole people. And this person I'm working with, who is important to me, appears to hate me. So I withdraw for a time, lick my wounds, think about what has happened. Sometimes I ask a friend from that culture to help me figure it out.

Gradually, I see my way out from under the avalanche. As the pain of the experience fades, I can usually see some truth in the accusation. Often I learn more about the accuser's painful relationships with my people in general than his or her relationship with me.

But in spite of my highest ideals, I still harbor attitudes that distance me from people who are different from me. These attitudes are part of our contextual baggage, and cannot just be wished away. The first step toward "unlearning" such attitudes is to recognize them in oneself. I've found questions like these helpful:

— Do I see aspects of beauty in this person? Am I repelled by the thought of touching this person in a reassuring or friendly way?

— Is my sense of humor unfettered when I'm with them? How do I feel when they are around my other friends? Is there anyone whose friendship I value who I feel should not see me with this person?

— Do I have anything that this person needs? How will I feel if they ask for it? Do they have anything I need? How will I feel if I have to ask them for it?

— How would I feel if this person were flying an airplane that I was in, or drilling my teeth? Do I make good eye contact with this person, or do I find my eyes wandering away to the furniture all the time?

— Do I secretly feel that I'm better, smarter, or more in control of my life than this person, and will therefore get my way if we have a disagreement? Do I secretly feel inferior, and expect that the other person will get his or her way?

Each of us carries such distancing attitudes within us, often unconsciously, and acts on them more or less often. They reflect the fear, suspicion, guilt, and anger that have developed over hundreds of years of oppression and separateness. My black lessons helped bridge some of these gaps for me. I think that the people my tutors took me to visit were especially enthusiastic because they were investing in the teacher of their community's children.

But reaching across centuries of painful experience is never easy. Many people are, understandably, reluctant to be spokespeople for their entire race, class, or group. Some have little confidence that such action would be worth the trouble. Facing the pain of the injustice they have endured, especially in the company of someone from a more privileged group, is often more than they want to do.

I HAVE BEGUN to understand how to harness the power of context. In my black lessons and American Willing to Listen project, I deliberately broadened my own context as a means to change my frame of reference and my behavior. At Sixth Street Park we worked together to craft a context which would support and sustain social consciousness.

In the largest sense, the aim of social movements is to change context, to shift the societal assumptions and expectations from which policies and practices arise. Slavery was once an accepted, widespread practice. Over time, the interplay between social and economic forces led to a contextual shift. Now slavery is not only illegal in most countries; the social context simply won't allow it.

The movements of our time—all the way from the campaign to stop drunk driving to the struggle for economic justice on a global scale or the work to abolish war—are striving to accomplish similar contextual changes. In time, it may become socially unacceptable to let a friend drive drunk, to exploit any country's workers and resources to enrich another country, or to settle political differences with force.

11 | Us and Them

TIME WAS WHEN I KNEW that the racists were the lunch-counter owners who refused to serve blacks, the warmongers were the generals who planned wars and ordered the killing of innocent people, and the polluters were the industrialists whose factories fouled the air, water, and land. I could be a good guy by boycotting, marching, and sitting-in to protest the actions of the bad guys.

But no matter how much I protest, an honest look at myself and my relationship with the rest of the world reveals ways that I too am part of the problem. I notice that on initial contact I am more suspicious of blacks or Mexicans than of white people. I see that I'm addicted to a standard of living maintained at the expense of poorer people around the world—a situation that can only be perpetuated through military force. And the problem of pollution seems to include my consumption of resources and creation of waste. The line that separates me from the bad guys is blurred.

WHEN I WAS WORKING to stop the Vietnam War, I'd feel uneasy seeing people in military uniform. I remember thinking, "How could that guy be so dumb as to have gotten into that uniform? How could he be so acquiescent, so credulous as to have fallen for the government's story on Vietnam?" I'd get furious inside when I imagined the horrible things he'd probably done in the war.

Several years after the end of the war, a small group of Vietnam veterans wanted to hold a retreat at our farm in Watsonville. I consented, although I felt ambivalent about hosting them. That weekend, I had a chance to listen to a dozen men and women who had served in Vietnam. Having returned home only to face ostracism for their involvement in the war, they were struggling to come to terms with their experiences.

They spoke of some of the awful things they'd done and seen, as well as some things they were proud of. They told why they had enlisted in the army or cooperated with the draft: their love of the United States, their eagerness to serve, their wish to be brave and heroic. They felt their noble motives had been betrayed, leaving them with little confidence in their own judgment. Now some questioned their own manhood or womanhood and even their basic humanity. They wondered whether they had been a positive force or a negative one overall. What meaning did their buddies' sacrifice have? Their anguish disarmed me, and I could no longer view them as simply perpetrators of evil.

How had I come to view military people as my enemy? Did vilifying soldiers serve to get me off the hook and allow me to divorce myself from responsibility for what my country was doing in Vietnam? Did my own anger and righteousness keep me from seeing the situation in its full complexity? How had this limited view affected my work against the war?

When my youngest sister and her husband, a young career military man, visited me several years ago, I was again challenged to see the human being within the soldier. I learned that as a farm boy in Utah, he'd been recruited to be a sniper.

One night toward the end of their visit, we got to talking about his work. Though he had also been trained as a medical corpsman, he could still be called on at any time to work as a sniper. He couldn't tell me much about this part of his career—he'd been sworn to secrecy. I'm not sure he would have wanted to tell me even if he could. But he did say that a sniper's work involved going abroad, "bumping off" a leader, and disappearing into a crowd.

When you're given an order, he said, you're not supposed to think about it. You feel alone and helpless. Rather than take on the Army and maybe the whole country himself, he chose not to consider the possibility that certain orders shouldn't be carried out.

I could see that feeling isolated can make it seem impossible to follow one's own moral standards and disobey an order. I leaned toward him and said, "If you're ever ordered to do something that you know you shouldn't do, call me immediately and I'll find a way to help. I know a lot of people would support your stand. You're not alone." He and my sister looked at each other and their eyes filled with tears.

Charlie and I performed our nuclear comedy show as a benefit for a peace group in San Diego, a city dominated by a huge naval base. During the intermission, a tall young man with a crewcut grabbed my hand and held it tightly as he asked, "What can we do to prevent nuclear war?" He was in college as part of his Navy training; in a few months he'd return to his job on a nuclear submarine. Responding to him, I said something about the importance of not killing people, but my answer seemed inadequate. His was a question I'd heard countless times, but never with such intensity. He was desperate to know what he could do.

HOW DO WE LEARN whom to hate and fear? During my short lifetime, the national enemies of the United States have changed several times. Our World War II foes, the Japanese and the Germans, have become our allies. The Russians have been in vogue as our enemy for some time, although during a few periods relations improved somewhat. The North Vietnamese, Cubans, and Chinese have done stints as our enemy. So many countries seem capable of incurring our national wrath—how do we choose among them?

As individuals, do we choose our enemies based on cues from

national leaders? From our schoolteachers and religious leaders? From newspapers and TV? Do we hate and fear our parents' enemies as part of our family identity? Or those of our culture, subculture, or peer group?

Whose economic and political interests does our enemy mentality serve?

AT THE CONFERENCE on holocaust and genocide I met someone who showed me that it is not necessary to hate our opponents, even under the most extreme circumstances. While sitting in the hotel lobby after a session on the Nazi holocaust, I struck up a conversation with a woman named Helen Waterford. When I learned she was a Jewish survivor of the Auschwitz concentration camp, I told her how angry I was at the Nazis for perpetrating the holocaust. (I guess I was trying to prove to her that I was one of the good guys.)

"You know," she said, "I don't hate the Nazis." This took me aback. How could anyone who had lived through a concentration camp not hate the Nazis?

Then I learned that Helen does public speaking engagements with a former leader of the Hitler Youth movement: they talk about how terrible fascism is as viewed from both sides.

Fascinated, I arranged to spend more time with Helen and learn as much as I could from her. After the end of World War II, she had emigrated to the United States. Then, in 1980, Helen read an intriguing newspaper article in which a man named Alfons Heck described his experiences growing up in Nazi Germany. When he was a young boy in Catholic school, the priest would come in every morning and say, "Heil Hitler," and then "Good morning," and finally "In the name of the Father and the Son and the Holy Spirit . . ." So in his mind Hitler came before God. At ten, Heck voluntarily joined the Hitler Youth, and he loved it. It was in 1944, when he was sixteen, that Heck first learned that the Nazis were systematically killing the Jews. He thought, "This can't be true." But gradually he came to believe that he had served a mass murderer.

Heck's frankness impressed Helen, and she thought, "I want to meet that man." She found him soft-spoken, intelligent, and pleasant. Helen had already been speaking publicly about her own experiences of the holocaust, and she asked Heck to share a podium with her at an upcoming engagement with a group of four hundred schoolteachers. They used a chronological format, taking turns telling their own stories of the Nazi period. Helen told of leaving Frankfurt in 1934 at age twenty-five. She and her husband, an accountant who had lost his job when the Nazis came to power, escaped to Holland. There they worked with the underground Resistance; Helen gave birth to their daughter. In 1940 the Nazis invaded Holland. Helen and her husband went into hiding in 1942. Two years later, they were discovered and sent to Auschwitz; their daughter was hidden by friends in the Resistance. Helen's husband died in the concentration camp.

Heck and Waterford's first joint presentation went well, and they decided to continue working as a team. Once, at an assembly of eight hundred high school students, Heck was asked, "If you had been ordered to shoot some Jews, maybe Mrs. Waterford, would you have shot them?" The audience gasped. Heck swallowed and said, "Yes. I obeyed orders. I would have." Afterward he apologized to Helen, saying he hadn't wanted to upset her. She told him, "I'm glad you answered the way you did. Otherwise, I would never again believe a word you said."

Heck is often faced with the "once a Nazi, always a Nazi" attitude. "You may give a good speech," people will say, "but I don't believe any of it. Once you have believed something, you don't throw it away." Again and again, he patiently explains that it took years before he could accept the fact that he'd been brought up believing falsehoods. Heck is also harassed by neo-Nazis, who call him in the middle of the night and threaten: "We haven't gotten you yet, but we'll kill you, you traitor."

How did Helen feel about the Nazis in Auschwitz? "I disliked them. I cannot say that I wished I could kick them to death—I never did. I guess that I am just not a vengeful person." She is often denounced by Jews for having no hate, for not wanting revenge. "It is impossible that you don't hate," people tell her.

At the conference and in subsequent conversations with Helen, I have tried to understand what has enabled her to remain so objective, to avoid blaming individual Germans for the holocaust, for her suffering and her husband's death. I have found a clue in her passionate study of history.

For many people, the only explanation of the holocaust is that it was the creation of a madman. But Helen believes that such an analysis only serves to shield people from believing that a holocaust could happen to them. An appraisal of Hitler's mental health, she says, is less important than an examination of the historical forces at play and the ways Hitler was able to manipulate them.

"As soon as the war was over," Helen told me, "I began to read about what had happened since 1933, when my world closed. I read and read. How did the 'S.S. State' develop? What was the role of Britain, Hungary, Yugoslavia, the United States, France? How can it be possible that the holocaust actually happened? What is the first step, the second step? What are people searching for when they join fanatical movements? I guess I will be asking these questions until my last days."

THOSE OF US WORKING for social change tend to view our adversaries as enemies, to consider them unreliable, suspect, and generally of lower moral character. Saul Alinsky, a brilliant community organizer, explained the rationale for polarization this way:

> One acts decisively only in the conviction that all the angels are on one side and all the devils are on the other. A leader may struggle toward a decision and weigh the merits and demerits of a situation which is 52 percent positive and 48 percent negative, but once the decision is reached he must assume that his cause is 100 percent positive and the opposition 100 percent negative. . . .
>
> Many liberals, during our attack on the then-school superintendent [in Chicago], were pointing out that after all he wasn't a 100 percent devil, he was a regular churchgoer, he was a good family man, and he was generous in his contributions to charity. Can you imagine in the arena of conflict charging that so-and-so is a racist bastard and then diluting the impact of the attack with qualifying remarks? This becomes political idiocy.

But demonizing one's adversaries has great costs. It is a strategy that tacitly accepts and helps perpetuate our dangerous enemy mentality.

Instead of focusing on the 52 percent "devil" in my adversary, I choose to look at the other 48 percent, to start from the premise that within each adversary I have an ally. That ally may be silent, faltering, or just hidden from my view. It may be only the person's sense of ambivalence about morally-questionable parts of his or her job. Such doubts rarely have a chance to flower because of the overwhelming power of the social context to which the person is accountable. *My* ability to be *their* ally also suffers from such pressures.

In 1970, while the Vietnam War was still going on, a group of us spent the summer in Long Beach, California, organizing against a napalm factory there. It was a small factory that mixed the chemicals and put the napalm in cannisters. An accidental explosion a few months before had spewed hunks of napalm gel onto nearby homes and lawns. The incident had, in a real sense, brought the war home. It spurred local residents who opposed the war to recognize their community's connection with one of its most despicable aspects. At their request, we worked with and strengthened their local group. Together we presented a slide show and tour of the local military-industrial complex for community leaders, and we picketed the napalm factory. We also met with the president of the conglomerate that owned the factory.

We spent three weeks preparing for this meeting, studying the company's holdings and financial picture and investigating whether there were any lawsuits filed against the president or his corporation. And we found out as much as we could about his personal life: his family, his church, his country club, his hobbies. We studied his photograph, thinking of the people who loved him and the people he loved, trying to get a sense of his worldview and the context he was accountable to.

We also talked a lot about how angry we were at him for the part he played in killing and maiming children in Vietnam. But though our anger fueled our determination, we decided that venting it at him would make him defensive and reduce our effectiveness.

When three of us met with him, he was not a stranger to us. Without blaming him personally or attacking his corporation, we asked him to close the plant, not to bid for the contract when it came up for renewal that year, and to think about the effects of what his company was doing. We told him we knew where his corporation was vulnerable (it owned a chain of motels that could be boycotted), and said we intended to continue working strategically to force his company out of the business of burning people. We also discussed the company's other war-related contracts, because changing just a small part of his corporation's functioning was not enough;

we wanted to raise the issue of economic dependence on munitions and war.

Above all, we wanted him to see us as real people, not so different from himself. If we had seemed like flaming radicals, he would have been likely to dismiss our concerns. We assumed he was already carrying doubts inside himself, and we saw our role as giving voice to those doubts. Our goal was to introduce ourselves and our perspective into his context, so he would remember us and consider our position when making decisions.

When the contract came up for renewal two months later, his company did not bid for it.

The victims of mercury poisoning in Minamata had several goals in their campaign: compensation for people suffering health damage, the establishment of a clinic, and a change in the factory's waste disposal procedures. But when they met with company officials, the victims' first demand was that the officials remember them in their prayers. They were appealing to the moral part of the officials' context.

Treating our opponents as bad guys may lead us to miss important information. After the International Hotel eviction, I found out that an undersheriff had lain awake nights worrying about the brutality he expected we would face from his partners in the eviction, the police. We hadn't listened to him closely enough when he had subtly tried to warn us in advance about the violence he foresaw. If we hadn't considered him "the enemy," we might have been alert to what he was saying and prepared more carefully for the police violence that occurred.

WORKING FOR SOCIAL CHANGE without relying on the concept of enemies raises some practical difficulties. For example, what do we do with all the anger that we're accustomed to unleashing against an enemy? Is it possible to hate actions and policies without hating the people who are implementing them? Does empathizing with those whose actions we oppose create a dissonance that undermines our determination?

I don't delude myself into believing that everything will work out for the best if I just make friends with my adversaries. I recognize that certain military strategists are making decisions that raise the risks for us all. I know that some police officers will rough up demonstrators when arresting them; some will habitually hurt people, and others use unnecessary force only when they're having a bad day. Treating our adversaries as potential allies need not entail unthinking acceptance of their actions. Our challenge is to call forth the humanity within each adversary, while at the same time preparing for the full range of possible responses. What path can we find between cynicism and naiveté?

12 | *Obstacles to Change*

CHANGE HAS ALWAYS fascinated me. Throughout my life I've tried to understand how change happens and what keeps it from happening. I have observed the dynamics of change in many areas. I have watched myself change personally: my work, my values, my lifestyle have gone through both sudden and gradual shifts. I have explored the learning and teaching processes, trying to understand how people change their ideas. As a counselor, I have watched people struggle to change aspects of their lives, battling to overcome blocks and painful experiences from the past. As a professional change agent, I have learned to help organizations get beyond the obstacles that are holding them back. And as a political activist, I have gathered

151

information about how societies change, how policy decisions affect the citizenry, and vice versa.

Over the years I have become dissatisfied with the assumptions upon which much change work is based. Between nations, within families, and in social change movements, there seems to be an unconscious assumption that effective change comes from imposing one's ideas on others. But I have found my work to be far more effective when I start from the premise that the change ideas and strategies appropriate to a situation are imbedded in the culture or group involved, waiting to be uncovered.

Nor do I accept the assumption that people are naturally apathetic, and the job of the social change agent is to motivate them. Instead, I work from the premise that each of us has within us the will to make the world a better place, as well as a longing for stability. We live in a tension between these two drives.

But there tend to be many more obstacles to our acting on the improvement impulse than to resting in inertia. So in my thinking I've shifted from the question "What makes people change?" to "What *keeps* people from changing?"

Most social change organizing focuses on "lack of information" as the key obstacle to change. The logic is that "if people only knew all the facts," the resulting outcry would set the necessary changes in motion. But I view the lack of information as only one among several kinds of obstacles. As we've seen, one's social context is a powerful force which can inhibit change: unquestioned assumptions about the way the world works can keep us from noticing the harmful consequences of the status quo. And, as the following stories show, many obstacles to working for change are emotionally-based.

A GOOD FRIEND OF MINE is, from all outward appearances, apathetic about the threat of nuclear war. Although she's been actively involved in civil rights and housing issues, and she recycles cans and bottles, she consistently avoids the nuclear issue. When we invite her to our nuclear comedy show, or when her son wants her to see a nuclear film, she finds reasons why she can't go. She has a cold, she's lost her umbrella, her favorite basketball team is playing, she's just too busy with errands. It's annoying, and I'm tempted to accuse her of not caring. One time she did volunteer to do some promotional work for our comedy show, but found she just couldn't get going on it. This baffled me: I'd worked with her before and had known her to be reliable and conscientious. At this point I could either assume that she was becoming lazy and irresponsible, or that there was some kind of obstacle in her way. In talking with her I suggested that her difficulties might have something to do with her feelings about nuclear war. She froze. She started shaking, and I saw sweat break out on her upper lip. After a few moments, she told me about a childhood experience that had terrified her. During World War II, her city had blackout drills at night—every building turned off all the lights so that the city would not be visible to potential enemy planes overhead. She was terrified of the dark but had to endure it. Every time she tried to face the nuclear issue, she was reminded of this terrifying experience. The pain was so great that she desperately tried to shield herself from the issue. That was the nature of her "apathy."

During the Vietnam War, I occasionally staffed a literature table in San Francisco for the Downtown Peace Coalition. Our goal was to convince office workers to work against the war. One day an ordinary-looking guy in a business suit came up and told me that he wouldn't attend our upcoming anti-war rally because, "I get so angry when I hear what they're doing in Vietnam that I'm afraid I'll lose my cool and punch someone."

It can be difficult to determine when someone is stuck because of an emotional obstacle, but I've learned to recognize signals in myself and others. People may get giddy, focus all their attention on minute details or semantics, get angry, avoid the issue, or seem to go numb—it's as if their emotions have scrambled their brain. They start grasping at straws—repeating something they heard on a talk show, or in school, or at the bridge club. It's no use trying to *convince* another person to abandon a position that is held in place by fear, anger, or hopelessness.

A group of environmentalists once asked me to help them with strategy. They had been fighting the damming of California's Stanislaus River for seven or eight years. Most active in the organization were the rafters, who spent summers and weekends on the river. Certain spots were particularly beloved to them. They told me about an old fig tree which had given them shade and juicy figs for years.

The river activists were a passionate bunch. Even after the dam had been constructed, they had lobbied, canvassed, and worked through legal channels to keep it from being put into operation. One man had chained himself to a boulder in the area that was to be flooded. But in spite of the activists' work, the back-river area had been partially flooded. Now they wanted to prevent the full flooding, but they were finding it impossible to think of strategies. And the more they berated one another for their paralysis, the more hopeless they became.

Talking with the group, I discovered that none of them had been to the river since the partial flooding had begun. They knew the area that had been flooded. Their old friend the fig tree was now under water. But even talking about the fig tree was too painful.

I began to understand why they couldn't devise strategies. By denying their feelings of disappointment in the face of defeat, they had gotten stuck. I sensed that they had to acknowledge and explore their pain in order to go forward. So, following the consultation, some of the rafters went back to their river. They saw the areas that were underwater and those that were still intact, and they said goodbye to the fig tree. Gradually, their energy and will returned; new strategies began to occur to them.

Emotional obstacles contain valuable information for the change agent. Instead of simply seeing individuals who are stuck, I've come to see my "apathetic" friend, the businessman who was too angry about the Vietnam War to protest against it, and the river activists as *representatives* of the fear, anger, and sadness that are present throughout society on these issues. Many people are too scared about nuclear war, too angry about intervention, too sad about our rivers, to do anything about these problems.

Ironically, those who seem most hopelessly stuck in emotional obstacles could, upon getting beyond them, make important contributions to the work for change. Who could take a more powerful stand against nuclear terror than someone who has known the deep fear of bombs? Who can speak better against an outrageous war than someone outraged by it?

Emotions not only keep us from working for change; they can also make the work we do less effective. Our best work is inspired by noble and natural feelings, like love for our children, our country, or the environment; fear of war; outrage at injustice and suffering. But harping on one's fear of war or screaming one's outrage at injustice will not necessarily be effective in bringing about change. It's important to accept and vent our feelings, but if we get stuck in this process and fail to think strategically about how to use our emotions, our work will be less than appropriate.

Our sense of urgency can also impair our effectiveness. We feel we must do something because something must be done, not because we know what is really appropriate to the situation.

Of course, action is absolutely necessary when we are confronted by a problem or condition that causes suffering. Nothing is more paralyzing than knowing what is wrong in the world without knowing what to do with that knowledge.

Allowing the suffering to ripen in one's soul is an essential component of appropriate action. One's feet move most determinedly when one's head and heart are both engaged.

OUR STRONGEST RESISTANCES to change are aroused when we are faced with new ideas or information. I learned a lot about this when trying to teach about gravity in science classes at Roosevelt Junior High School. By the eighth grade, most kids have unconsciously created their own explanation of gravity. Many have concluded that there is a magnet at the core of the earth—another invisible force they've observed. It was difficult for me to teach about gravity until these old assumptions had been aired. If I started out by saying, "This pencil falls down because of the gravitational pull of the earth, which is the combination of centripetal and centrifugal forces," most students just wouldn't understand or believe me.

So instead, I'd begin the gravity lesson by asking, "Why does this pencil fall?" and then I'd survey the class for explanations, acknowledging each person's hypothesis. As we discussed and tested these explanations, weaknesses became apparent. Where *is* the magnet? What is the magnetic substance in the pencil? Only after this process would we explore alternative ideas, including the generally-accepted theory of gravity. It didn't answer all of the questions, but it covered more than the old explanations did and led to deeper questions.

The time between the awareness of the old idea's inadequacy and the finding of a more satisfactory idea is a time of tension. For some people, the tension is unbearable. How could they have been so foolish as to believe something which is now not the best answer?

When I first heard the idea that the United States should get its troops out of Vietnam, I reacted against it. And at first I refused to believe the reports that our food was contaminated with pesticides. Gradually, as I gathered more information, I came to believe both these ideas. Although I have changed my ideas many times, I still have difficulty dealing with new ones.

Living in California, I'm constantly confronted with new ideas: reincarnation, acupuncture, divine light healing, prosperity training, or the one where you put food in your bellybutton, hold your arm out, and let people test your strength. (If you can resist their pushing your arm down, the food's supposed to be good for you.) Many of these ideas are somewhat inconsistent with my scientific training, my Idaho background, and what I have always thought of as my good common sense.

My mind boggles as the new idea comes in. How could an intelligent person whom I care about be suggesting such silly, outlandish things? A sheepish grin comes over me; I begin to chuckle inside. I know I'm not supposed to laugh out loud because this person is serious about acupuncture or divine light healing, but waves of silliness come over me as my old ideas slip and fall on the banana peel of a new idea. (I leave it to you to guess which ideas mentioned above I have come to believe in, wholly or partially.)

I've surely carried more than my share of wild ideas into other people's lives: laughing about nuclear war, raising chickens in my backyard in San Francisco, shaving my head just for the fun of it, building a park for street people. I've noticed that some people tend to accept new ideas readily, while others are more cautious.

Change theorist Everett Rogers divides people into five categories: innovators, early adopters, early majority, late majority, and laggards. Innovators, a small percentage of any group, are the designers of new ideas; they are the "loose marbles," those who are already considered "different" and have less to lose by taking risks and challenging the norm. Early adopters are closer to the mainstream of the culture; they act as the conduit carrying the new ideas to others. Those in the early and late majority groups are progressively more skeptical, tending to value stability over change. The laggards are most resistant to change; I think of them as chronically terrified. But without the late majority and the laggards, we might careen into every new idea full tilt.

You can't tell who's in which category by outward appearances, but there tend to be patterns in the ways individuals react to new ideas. One can sometimes predict an individual's response and introduce a new idea accordingly. People do react slightly differently, influenced by such factors as their sense of security, their economic interest, the nature of the new idea, and how it's presented.

It's interesting, and sometimes even fun, to watch people reject ideas. I've come to see resistance as a valuable component of the change process, not merely an obstacle to overcome. It helps me test ideas and see some of their weaknesses.

Sometimes I can get a sense of the power of an idea based on the force people put into resisting it. When I first met Mahantji and suggested that the Ganga River could be saved, his resistance was absolute. The deep hopelessness I sensed in him gave me a clue about how powerfully this change might affect the Indian people. To make progress in this seemingly hopeless task would radically expand the boundaries of what they considered possible.

IT IS NOT ONLY my "Idaho optimism" that makes me assume people have an internal drive for improvement. I find that this stance is also quite practical. It has served me in many different situations.

One year I worked as an educational consultant at Everett Junior High School in San Francisco. Among the teachers the principal asked me to work with were some he considered "major problems." Although I had my own ideas about what these teachers needed to change, I put those ideas aside and asked each teacher, "What do you want to improve about your teaching?"

I was surprised that, for the most part, the teachers wanted to improve in the same areas that I saw as weaknesses. One teacher wanted to keep from venting her anger at the students. Another eventually confided to me that he wanted to stop coming to school drunk. Others wanted new ideas for getting the students to work together cooperatively; some wanted help with specific instructional techniques. I had established myself as their ally, which allowed us to work together on their goals. Had I come to them insisting on the same changes, they would have been likely to defend themselves

against my criticisms. It would have been more difficult for them
to change.

At Sixth Street Park I began with the assumption that the street
people wanted a park that would work beautifully for everyone involved.
Some people feared that if we built a park for street people, they
would just turn it into Hoodlum City. Had we operated on that view,
we would have designed the park defensively. We would have put
fences around all the trees. We wouldn't have given staff members
keys to the tool shed. The park would have been completely paved,
to make it less vulnerable to vandalism.

Instead, we created a place that expressed confidence in the park
users, a place of beauty and utility. We built benches wide enough
for people to sleep on. It's true, some of the trees didn't survive. That
was part of the cost. But in general, the park remained well cared for.

In the campaign to save the Ganga, we could assume that the
people of Varanasi pollute their river because they fundamentally
don't care about it. Based on that assumption, we might try to cajole,
shock, or otherwise manipulate them into becoming concerned. Instead,
we assume that people do care, that the plight of the river causes them
pain, and that they would like to do something to help improve the
situation.

The "whole truth" is that a part of each of us says, "The Ganga
must be clean," and another part has found a way to live with the
pollution on a day-to-day basis. So the change agent's task is to
acknowledge the latter while building a campaign based on the
former.

FACILITATING THE CHANGE PROCESS is like sculpting a block of
wood. Although we who envision the change may have images of the
results we want, we do not have control; there is interplay with the
wood. Our primary task as change agents is to "raise the grain" of the
material we're working with, to uncover the ideas and symbols that
will contribute to the change strategy.

In this process, I have come to rely heavily on listening and
questioning. As a listener, I try to give people a chance to explore an
issue openly; I focus on the aspects that are unresolved or painful to
them, and on their hopes and visions of how the situation could be

different. This allows ideas to emerge that can become the seeds of strategy.

The quality of my research is directly affected by the nature of my questions. Open-ended, non-judgmental questions are most likely to open new avenues. "Where are the women?" for example, is a much more appropriate question than, "Don't you think you should have women in this campaign?" or, "What's the matter with these women that they don't get involved?"

Listening is not the same as silence. It does not imply that as a listener, I lack clear ideas or positions of my own. In fact, the clearer I am about my own perspective, the less I need constant confirmation of it from others. My opinions come with me, but I can choose not to pay attention to them. When my goal is to give the other person an opportunity to explore an issue, inserting my opinions is usually inappropriate. To do so would change the dialogue; the person I'm listening to would react to my views, either by saying things they would expect me to agree with, or those that might provoke me. When asked for my opinion, I try to offer it lightly, not to persuade but to encourage further dialogue.

Some interesting experiments using these techniques are being undertaken by "citizen diplomacy" projects in several countries. One group doing such work is the small U.S.-based Mo Tzu Project (named after a Chinese peacemaker of the fifth century B.C.). Members travel to an area of conflict and meet one-on-one with members of the parties to the conflict, asking them to explain the situation as they see it. Taking the stance of impartial but concerned outsiders, they listen patiently and attentively, often enduring passionate speeches about the righteousness of a particular cause. They ask open-ended questions. To a Palestinian leader: "Under what circumstances would the PLO recognize Israel?" To an Israeli: "What would enable the Israeli government to agree to a Palestinian homeland?" Having already been given a thorough hearing, the disputants may feel sufficiently understood to explore these questions creatively, to acknowledge doubts they have about their own position, and to give voice to new ideas.

The interviewers create a relatively neutral social environment—one in which closed questions can be reopened and new possibilities considered. Their aim is to discover complementarity in the positions of the conflicting parties. Recognizing this, the parties become less righteous, belligerent, and defensive. Bob Fuller, one of the pioneering Mo Tzu interviewers, writes: "Our goal is to look together for at least a theoretical solution—one which would leave all parties with their self-respect, and each with a sense that they own a piece of the truth, while glimpsing the possibility of owning a larger truth by incorporating that of the other side." Even after the interviewers have left, the sense of new possibilities remains with the disputants.

One of the frustrations in Mo Tzu work, as in all listening work, is that the results can never be conclusively ascertained. "We are constantly aware of how small our contribution is relative to the size and seriousness of the problems in which we're immersed," Bob says. "But it's like throwing a stone into a lake: you don't see the water level rise, but you know the stone is sitting at the bottom, so you conclude that the water level must have risen. When we have done well by a situation, we sense that the water level has risen."

I once heard a story about how Tibetan Buddhists handle ghosts. If a family or village is having a problem, such as an onslaught of grasshoppers, or illness, or too much bickering, then the local monastery is asked to send a lama to get rid of the ghost who is causing these problems. The lama comes to the village, and goes from house to house listening to people talk about everything that has been going on, listening to the most unrelated information, listening beyond the point when an ordinary person would stop listening. And still he listens more.

When everyone has been heard, the lama goes back to the monastery, thinks about what he has heard, the people and their stories, and weaves a ghost trap out of yarn. The trap is made of triangles similar to Mexican god's eyes, except they are three-dimensional. He makes one large trap—occasionally as large as six feet high—and some smaller traps. At the end of each structural part of the large trap he attaches a little ball of white cotton. Finally he makes some little doors out of flat pieces of wood. Now he is ready to go back to the village and trap the ghost.

The lama finds an appropriate crossroads, makes a mound of mud, and sticks the trap upright into the mound. Around the large trap, he places the small traps and doors in a circle. The theory is that the ghost comes along the road and is a bit distracted by the crossroads. He sees the doors (ghosts evidently love to sneak around closed doors) and, avoiding the little traps, gets stuck in the large one. Meanwhile, the lama has been sitting nearby praying and meditating, and he comes out every now and then to pinch the little cotton balls. When they are wet, he knows that the ghost is trapped. He plucks the trap out of the ground, carries it to a cliff, and flings it over. Now, according to the belief, the ghost has been removed, and life will return to normal.

Since I first heard this story, it has seemed strikingly similar to some of my ideas about how to make social change. What interests me is not the building of the ghost trap, but the transforming nature of the lama's listening.

As a change agent, I can identify with the lama. I begin my work by interviewing everyone involved. I try to look at the problem in its relationship to the entire social environment, paying attention even to those elements that may not seem directly relevant. I let the information I gather occupy me fully. Then I reflect on my understanding of history and innovation theory. I also examine my dreams, idle musings, and common-sense hunches. It is only after this period of examination and contemplation that I "weave" my recommendation.

I have always wondered what would happen if I didn't return with recommendations for the organization. What would be the effect of the deep listening alone? Might the necessary changes occur as a result of the consultation process itself?

IN MY OWN LIFE, I know I change more effectively when people work with me to overcome my problems rather than banging me over the head and saying: "Change! Change, already!" It is a paradox that the goals of the change agent, born of high ideals and the noble drive for improvement, can actually interfere with or subvert the change process.

There is no work that I have found more connecting and fulfilling than helping other people to remove obstacles in their path to change. From San Francisco schoolteachers to people on the banks of the Ganga, I have seen the human will to improve, to make our lives and our world more convergent with our ideals. I know the pain that comes from not being able to translate this will into reality.

13 | Tales of Change

MY FRIEND and colleague Joanna Macy relates a story based on the Shambhala prophecy found in Tibetan Buddhism. The following interpretation was told to Joanna by the Tibetan lama Choegyal Rinpoche:

> We are now entering a time of extreme danger in which two great powers—called *lalös*, or barbarians—are locked in mutual hostility. One is in the center of the Eurasian land mass, the other is in the West, and they have, for all their enmity, a great deal in common, including the fact that they have both developed and are manufacturing and deploying weapons of unfathomable death and devastation.
>
> So the future of the planet is in question. And it is at this time that the kingdom of Shambhala begins to emerge. This kingdom is

hard to detect because it is not a geopolitical entity; it exists in the hearts and minds of the "Shambhala warriors." For that matter, you can't even recognize Shambhala warriors by looking at them—they wear no insignias, badges, or uniforms; they carry no banners; they have no barricades behind which to rest or regroup, no turf to call their own. Ever and always they do their work on the terrain of the *lalös* themselves.

There comes a time, which we are now approaching, when physical and moral courage is required of these Shambhala warriors. They must go right into the centers and corridors of power, into the very citadels where these weapons—in the broadest sense of the term—are kept. There they must dismantle these weapons. Now is the time that the Shambhala warriors must train for this work. They train in the use of two weapons. One is compassion—the intense tuning to the sufferings of others. The other is a clear understanding of our profound mutuality, interconnectedness, and complicity—the web of being in which we all coexist. Without either of these weapons courage will falter and burn out, strategies become confused, actions too partisan.

For me, this prophecy is a powerful fable of change. It describes conflicts both in the outer world and within myself—the internal battle between my barbarian nature and my compassionate nature. And the "no badges" idea reminds me that it is folly to put on the badge of a "good guy warrior." That may serve the ego's need for self-definition, but it does not serve the challenge of our time. It divides us from other people, allowing us to withdraw behind a barricade of righteousness. As Joanna puts it, "If there are any battle lines to distinguish the good guys from the bad, they traverse the internal landscape of each individual."

TALES LIKE THIS ONE can offer us images of the change process and insight into our own "changeview"—our ideas about how change happens. Just as each of us has a unique worldview, so we have a unique changeview. It comes from what we've been taught about change, our understanding of history, and our own observations and experiences. Most of the time our changeview remains unconscious, but making it conscious gives us a basis for designing our work for change.

There is no such thing as a complete changeview, or a correct one. Our changeviews need to be constantly tested and revised, the way a kid tests a new toy—by throwing it against the wall, chewing on it, tearing off the cover and seeing what's inside.

Writing this book has been that kind of process for me. It has forced me to consider my view of change and how it has evolved. It has made me think about changes I've made in my life, as well as changes I've seen in the world around me. Seeing my grandmother hug a black man, participating with thousands of people in the defense of the International Hotel, traveling around the world to listen to ordinary people—these experiences have expanded the boundaries of what I consider possible.

I've had to ask myself which parts of my changeview I drew from my parents' values, and which parts I developed in reaction to those values.

How does my position in the world—my race, class, gender, nationality, family situation—affect my changeview? How does the fact that I'm white contribute to my optimism? Would I be so sanguine about the future if I were an American Indian and saw my culture disappearing? As a middle-class American addicted to creature comforts, I find certain changes threatening even to contemplate. On the other hand, my fatness has given me valuable distance from the accepted norms of American womanhood and may have helped me be more open-minded about considering changes.

One's changeview is deeply influenced by the interpretation of history one accepts. In school, my history books implied that national change was a function of war: which wars a country won and which it lost. It's taken me a long time, and a lot of reading and thinking, to come to a new, more complex analysis—one which includes the possibility of large-scale change without war.

The social changes I've read about—the abolition of slavery, the unionization of factory workers, the American revolution and revolutions in other countries: what is my understanding of how they occurred? And what lessons do I draw from the social change movements I've participated in, like the civil rights movement? Although racism is still alive and well, I do see more whites and blacks acting friendly toward each other on the bus. Our society expects that now, at least more so than it did twenty years ago. What made that change possible? What kept it from going further? I think about the sacrifices involved: the people who spent hours stuffing envelopes and walking precincts, as well as those who were murdered for their support of the cause.

Any American old enough to remember the Vietnam War has

his or her own ideas, held consciously or unconsciously, about what finally caused the United States to withdraw from the war. One conclusion I drew was that in order for a massive social structure to make a change, it takes people working toward the same general goal from many different points of view, with many different analyses, strategies, and tactics. It takes groups working on demonstrations, legal challenges, legislative lobbying, entertainment, prayer, education, funding, media work, and so on. I lovingly call this the "niche theory" of social change, though it is more precisely a postulate, an assumption which I have found useful. It reminds me, for example, that in working to prevent nuclear war, certain groups whose strategies make no sense to me, may in fact be making key contributions. It helps me see these people as my collaborators, rather than my competitors.

AS ONE'S CHANGEVIEW EVOLVES, new stories and images become significant. In my travels, I hear particular stories and images referred to again and again—new tales that fuel people's work for change. In 1984, I don't know how many times I heard someone say, "You know, it only took ten percent of the population to make the American Revolution." Activists who felt outnumbered by "nonbelievers" seemed to find this concept heartening.

In the early eighties many people working to prevent nuclear war found the hundredth monkey story empowering. As the story goes, scientists observing monkeys on several small islands would drop sweet potatoes in the sand for the monkeys. A young monkey discovered that she could wash the sand off in a stream; she taught her mother and her playmates, who in turn taught their mothers. Over a period of years, all the young monkeys on the island, as well as some of the older ones, learned about washing the sweet potatoes. One morning, when a certain number of monkeys, say ninety–nine, knew how to wash the sweet potatoes, the hundredth monkey learned how. By that evening, almost all the monkeys were washing their sweet potatoes—and those on other islands spontaneously began doing so. The hundredth monkey's choice to wash the sand off made the critical difference.

This story functioned as a kind of new version of the David and Goliath story. But instead of teaching that "you can win and be a hero in face of overwhelming odds," the hundredth monkey suggested that "your contribution just might be the crucial link."

Of the stories that contribute to my changeview, some are ancient, traditional ones like the Shambhala warrior prophesy. Some are stories I read or hear about. Others are stories based on my own experience. I include here some of my favorite ones, along with the ideas they help me keep in mind.

Deborah Lubar's Listening Story

A friend of mine, Deborah Lubar, wrote a moving account of a door-to-door listening exercise. Her task was to find out what people were thinking, rather than trying to convince them of anything. Pad in hand, she introduced herself and asked the following questions:

What do you think is the greatest problem facing the world today? What do you consider the chances of nuclear war to be? Do you discuss these concerns with your family, friends, or colleagues? What do you think would make our country safe and strong?

One man who grudgingly let her into his house turned hostile when she asked him about nuclear war. He barked, "No, no, no, no! I don't have time for these ridiculous questions." She left, feeling stung by his rudeness. A few minutes later, as she was coming out of another house, there the man stood, with his arms crossed, waiting for her.

"What do you expect me to *do* about it?" he demanded belligerently. "I'm sorry I threw you out of my house, but what in hell do you expect me to do about it? For God's sake, what do you want?" They went for a walk. He pelted her with questions about her survey and about nuclear war, deterrence, and defense policy; finally he shook her hand and walked away.

The next morning, Deborah followed an impulse and went back to the man's house. She felt like a fool—what excuse could she give for returning? Finally she just went to the door. The man answered, surprised but glad to see her. He told her that he'd had a horrible night, sweating through nightmares about nuclear war. He recounted his dreams in vivid detail; when she leaned over to touch his hand, he started to weep. After a while his sadness gave way to rage at his sense of helplessness as a human being on a planet headed for disaster. He bashed his fist on the table and shouted, "What a world! It's a misery and a burden to be a human being!"

Deborah says, "That moment was agony for me." She wanted to assure him that there was another side, that human beings do have the power to change the situation. "But I knew enough to keep still. Who was I to tell him such a thing? Although what he had said was only *part* of the truth, it was part of the truth. His rage was just; I had no right to argue with its power."

They talked of many things, until the man realized he was late for work. At the door he took her hands and they looked each other straight in the eye. "What we learned of one another that morning," writes Deborah, "was profoundly intimate, and yet it had *only* to do with our common bond as two human beings groping in the dark to confront and move through the difficult times we live in."

I've had experiences similar to Deborah Lubar's, though none as dramatic. Her story gives me a picture of what it means to stick with someone beyond the anger and rejection; it helps me see people's anger and pain as expressions of deep caring rather than of not caring. The taboo against talking about nuclear war and other painful issues has created chasms between people and has kept us from sharing some of the deepest parts of our human experience. Listening openheartedly and asking opening questions can often unlock the areas that have been tightly bolted down by fear and social pressures.

This story also helps me remember that outbursts of anger that appear to be directed at the person who brings up a painful subject may really reflect anger about the subject itself. (This is true of other strong feelings as well.) Listening to the outburst, not taking it personally, can help the other person move through it.

It was important that when the man kicked her out, Deborah didn't challenge him, didn't push him beyond where he was willing to go. She let him stay in control, she withdrew, but she did not give up on him.

C.P. Ellis and Ann Atwater

One of the oral histories Studs Terkel presents in his book *American Dreams: Lost and Found* is that of C.P. Ellis. Ellis grew up in Durham, North Carolina, the son of a textile worker who died at forty-eight of brown lung. As a young father of four, C.P. found he was barely able to support his own family. "I worked my butt off and just never seemed to break even," he remembered. "I really began to get bitter. I didn't know who to blame. I had to hate somebody. The natural person for me to hate would be black people, because my father before me was a member of the Klan. As far as he was concerned, it was the savior of the white people."

Ellis joined the Ku Klux Klan ("It was a thrilling moment"), and rose to become president of the Durham chapter. Then he was thrust into a working relationship with Ann Atwater, a black civil rights leader.

A Klansman and a militant black woman, co-chairmen of the school committee. It was impossible. How could I work with her? . . . Her and I began to reluctantly work together. She had as many problems workin' with me as I had workin' with her.

. . . I said: "If we're gonna make this thing a success, I've got to get to my kind of people." The low-income whites. We walked the streets of Durham, and we knocked on doors and invited people. Ann was goin' into the black community. They just wasn't respondin' to us when we made these house calls. Some of 'em were cussin' us out. "You sellin' us out, Ellis, get out of my door. I don't want to talk to you." Ann was gettin' the same response from blacks: "What are you doin' messin' with that Klansman?"

One day, Ann and I went back to the school and we sat down. We began to talk and just reflect. Ann said: "My daughter came home cryin' every day. She said her teacher was makin' fun of me in front of the other kids." I said: "Boy, the same thing happened to my kid. White liberal teacher was makin' fun of Tim Ellis's father, the Klansman. In front of other peoples. He came home cryin'." At this point I begin to see, here we are, two people from the far ends of the fence, havin' identical problems, except hers bein' black and me bein' white. From that moment on, I tell ya, that gal and I worked together good. I begin to love the girl, really. *(He weeps.)*

C.P. Ellis and Ann Atwater remind me that connection is never impossible, no matter what the social climate, no matter how unlikely it seems. It was an act of heroism on both of their parts to accept the other's hand in friendship—especially considering that both were public figures. By responding defensively, either could have easily prevented the other from reaching across. This picture helps me keep going.

They also remind me that when you start getting connected to people who are different, you should prepare yourself for criticism, resistance, and perhaps hostility from those around you.

The story causes me to wonder whether, when people are acting in the most overtly racist way, they are actually longing for help in getting beyond their prejudice.

Stanley Milgram's Experiments on Disobedience

Psychological researcher Stanley Milgram conducted a series of experiments in which subjects were asked to teach another person to memorize a series of paired words. When the learner made a mistake, the subject was to push a button to administer electric shocks of progressively higher voltages until the shocks were clearly at a dangerous level. (No shocks were actually being administered, and the "learner" was really an actor who would feign physical responses to electroshock.)

An overwhelming majority of the subjects continued administering shocks until the experiment ended, obeying authority in spite of their certainty that the shocks were causing the learner serious harm.

One lesson I draw from Milgram's work is that contextual pressures can cause us to override even our most basic values. None of us is incapable of doing horrible things. This seems consistent with the observations about holocaust and genocide that I heard at the conference in Tel Aviv. Ordinary people like you and me, people whom you'd expect to be able to think independently and take a stand, can do evil. This willingness to go along, even to the point of harming others, isn't an aberration. We are all well–practiced in doing as we are told, doing what seems appropriate to the context. As human beings, we must face up to this problem and find ways to compensate for it.

Milgram's experiments also have important ramifications for my thinking about connectedness. He found that people are less likely to continue the torture if they are in the same room as the victim than if they are kept separate. So when we see our society scapegoating particular groups of people, it's important that we bring ourselves closer to them. In 1980, when I knew that Iranians in the United States were being harassed and beaten up, I found myself wondering how we could establish human connections between Iranians and others in the United States. How can we protect ourselves as a society from persecuting particular racial or cultural groups?

My third lesson from Milgram's research is: If you're going to disobey, there are more and less effective ways of doing it. In one variation of the experiment, Milgram had two people at the electroshock controls. (Both were presumably subjects but one was actually another actor working in cahoots with Milgram.) When the shocks got to the dangerous level, the confederate refused to continue administering shocks, leaving the subject to take over. Milgram discovered that a crucial distinction was whether the disobedient person left the room at this point, or stayed and watched. The subject was much more likely to refuse to harm the learner if the disobedient person remained present, a moral witness to the subject's actions.

Luisa Delacruz at the Bank, and the American Lawyer in China

While I was fighting eviction at the International Hotel, one of the tenants died, and Luisa Delacruz, another tenant, was named executor of his will. She asked me to accompany her to the bank to help with a complex transaction. As it turned out, we either didn't have the proper forms, or the bank had a policy against doing what Luisa needed to do. The manager explained the problem cordially to her.

"There must be a way," Luisa said to him. "I have his will here. I am the executor, and I need to get the money for funeral expenses." The manager explained that it couldn't be done. She said, "It has to be done." He walked away.

So Luisa just sat there at the manager's desk, and the two of us chatted. We must have waited there for about an hour. I couldn't fathom Luisa's strategy. Finally, the manager returned and said, "Oh, all right," and he did what she had asked. I was in awe—I had never seen a "no" turned into a "yes" that way. By maintaining our presence without forcing a confrontation with the manager, she allowed him to change his mind.

When I went to China in 1974, our tour group had to stay there longer than we had planned. Japan Airlines' workers were on strike, and in support of the strike, the Chinese government wouldn't allow us to patronize the airline. A lawyer in our group had to get back to the United States for an important hearing, and he mounted a personal campaign to pressure our Chinese tour guides into granting him an exception. It culminated in his screaming and shouting at the tour guides in the hotel lobby, threatening lawsuits, and using every power ploy he could think of. The guides were uncharacteristically relaxed in the situation, and even laughed. They said, "These threats are meaningless here."

We Westerners assume that in order to get our way we either have to be ingratiating, or we have to build pressure. In China, I could see how ridiculous this pressure-building approach appeared to people in another culture.

Luisa showed me that there is power in simply maintaining a calm, unyielding presence, that constantly increasing pressure is not the only way to act in the face of an obstacle. Her calmness did not communicate lack of determination. It communicated confidence that the bank manager would come to see the reasonableness of her request.

I also love this story because it reminds me that the people close to us can inspire us and provide us with models of change.

Building Confidence

When I was in Beijing, I asked people what the Chinese revolution had been like for those who lived there. The People's Liberation Army had encircled Beijing, so people couldn't take the garbage and night soil out, and couldn't bring food in. It was a time of hardship. I asked what made people believe in the PLA during the revolution. Several told me a similar story:

"We had been conquered many times," they told me, "—by the Mongols, the Japanese, by various Chinese armies. Each time, the conquerors would march through our city, commandeer our municipal buildings, take all the treasures out of the temples, come into our homes, and force us to sleep in the streets. But the PLA marched in at night, quietly. When I woke up in the morning, I looked outside and the soldiers were sleeping in the streets. They did not loot our homes, stores, or temples. They had discipline. They helped us clean up the city. Instead of ordering us to take the trash out, they helped us take it out. We could tell that these people were interested in our problems. We had confidence in them."

In Varanasi, I noticed that the people who had been part of the Gandhian movement for India's independence always come to meetings on time. At the appointed hour, they are predictably sitting in their places, focused on the task, ready to go. Leela, one of the women, explained to me: "We had to be on time. We Indians have a reputation for being late. But we had to have enough self-discipline to get done what we needed to." She told me that Gandhi would say, "I will give you fifteen minutes of my time, from 2:00 to 2:15." If you showed up ten minutes late, you would get only five minutes. At 2:15 he would turn his attention to other matters.

To me, the People's Liberation Army story says: Large-scale change is very frightening. But if those who are identified with the change are exemplary human beings, if they don't abuse their power and position, others are more likely to have confidence in them and to support the change they're promoting. By sleeping in the streets and taking on a share of the dirty work, the PLA exemplified the change they were fighting for: a system of government that served the interests of the common people.

The Gandhian story reminds me that people trust and take seriously people who have self-discipline, who do what they say they're going to do. Groups need to have control of themselves in order to have the confidence that they can accomplish their goals. If we can't start the meeting when we said we would, how can we hope to prevent nuclear war? Groups need to start by doing little things well, so as to have confidence in themselves and each other, and to build a reputation in the larger community for being trustworthy. Although the idea of discipline seems to be unpopular these days, purposeful self-discipline can be meaningful and empowering.

The Hallelujah Chorus

Easter is a big deal in Twin Falls, and every year our whole family went to church together. I'll never forget the Easter when I was sixteen, and sang in the choir at the First Presbyterian Church. The first service was really crowded; there must have been three hundred people there. The whole service was glorious. The minister finished his sermon, put his hands up for the benediction, and all of us in the choir stood up to sing the Hallelujah Chorus. It was very exciting.

So we were singing along, "Hallelujah! Hallelujah!" We got to the very end of the chorus, where it goes: "Hallelujah! (eighth–note rest) Hallelujah! (eighth–note rest) Hallelujah!" and then there are two *quarter*–note rests. But I took only an eighth rest, so in my loud voice, I sang "Haaaa" too early. By the time everyone else came in with "Haa," I had stopped singing. I turned bright red, which was quite a contrast to my blue choir gown.

There was an hour break between the first service and the second service, and I sneaked out of the church, went home, and put on my bluejeans. I thought: "I can't go back to that church. I'll just become a Methodist." But when my father found out, he insisted that I go upstairs, change into my church clothes, and go back to church. He stood firm. "Never run away from things you're afraid of," he said. So I went back to the second service, and I sang. When we came to the "Hallelujah!" part, I mouthed the words just to be on the safe side.

To this day, I still feel afraid at that point in the music, but this story helps me remember that I can survive making a mistake in public. It reminds me that my mistakes are a step on the road of change, experiences to learn from and move beyond. This perspective allows me to take risks more freely, and helps me see myself as a fundamentally good person even when I make a mistake.

It also helps me view other people's mistakes with compassion. Each of us has areas of great strength and areas where we consistently perform poorly and should not be relied on. One of my weakest areas is bookkeeping. I wouldn't steal, but I'm not exactly noted for my clerical ability, so I would never be able to prove that money hadn't been misappropriated. I don't think it would be worth the effort to retrain me in this area. My rule of thumb is that most of us are out of our depth about twelve percent of the time, whether or not we realize it. Fortunately, our areas of inability differ, so that people working together can cover for each other.

The Fanmaker and the Phone Worker

Before visiting China, I was disturbed to learn that in China individuals don't choose their jobs but are assigned to them by the government. What if I lived there and was assigned to be an elevator operator! How could I be satisfied spending my life that way?

This issue continued to gnaw at me during our tour. One day, we visited a fanmakers' workshop. I talked with a woman whose work was to stretch fabric over a wire frame, glue the two together, and then paint goldfish on the fabric. "Do you like your work?" I asked her. "Oh yes," she said. "Before the revolution I worked alone in my home. I couldn't talk to other fanmakers. Now we meet and decide what to do with these fans." I asked what value she saw in her work. "These fans are sent to the Philippines, Hong Kong, or Singapore," she replied. "They bring in foreign currency which allows our country to buy the things we need from other countries. And people enjoy these fans and feel friendly toward my country. These fans are making friends for China."

I stubbornly persisted. "Don't you sometimes wish you could do work that would be more valuable to your society?" At this point our tour guide became impatient. She turned to me and asked: "Do you consider *my* work valuable?" Yes, I said. She said, "Well, my work is no more important than my sister the fanmaker's. She and I are working for China together."

This story brings to mind a secretary from the phone company whom I once met. "How can I feel like I'm contributing to the world?" she said. "All I do every day is figure out how much tax the phone company should pay for stringing transmission lines across public property."

In our society, individuals' work tends to be measured in terms of profit and productivity. We rarely perceive each person's work as an intrinsically valuable contribution to society. To compensate for this, I think of the fanmaker and the tour guide, and the way they view their work and each other's—as small but important parts of a whole.

The Chimpanzee at Stanford

One day I was walking through the Stanford University campus with a friend when I saw a crowd of people with cameras and video equipment on a little hillside. They were clustered around a pair of chimpanzees—a male running loose and a female on a chain about twenty-five feet long. It turned out the male was from Marine World and the female was being studied for something or other at Stanford. The spectators were scientists and publicity people trying to get them to mate.

The male was eager. He grunted and grabbed the female's chain and tugged. She whimpered and backed away. He pulled again. She pulled back. Watching the chimps' faces, I began to feel sympathy for the female.

Suddenly the female chimp yanked her chain out of the male's grasp. To my amazement, she walked through the crowd, straight over to me, and took my hand. Then she led me across the circle to the only other two women in the crowd, and she joined hands with one of them. The three of us stood together in a circle. I remember the feeling of that rough palm against mine. The little chimp had recognized us and reached out across all the years of evolution to form her own support group.

This story reminds me how much we need support from others who understand our position, who can empathize with us.

I remember listening in on my parents' bridge club when I was young. All they seemed to talk about was their children. Now I wonder: Was the goal of the club to play bridge or to have a chance to talk about the problems they were having with their kids and get their friends' thinking and support? They were accountable to that group. They knew that the next time they saw each other, they would be asked: "How did Miriam's problem at school work out?"

We don't all have bridge clubs, and often must, like the chimp, invent the support structures we need. I don't think I would be able to sustain my work against such a formidable opponent as nuclear war without an ongoing support group. The group helps us all work through emotional blocks, and nourishes and challenges us intellectually.

Every now and then I have run up against a brick wall in my efforts to understand my work and my life. Thoughts of giving up fill my days. When it seems almost impossible to go on, I call up five or six trusted friends and ask them to form an "emergency committee." I agree to do whatever they ask me to do. The group gathers, and I sketch out for them the problem in all its financial, emotional, and interpersonal dimensions. They question me, and when they feel they fully understand the situation, I leave the room and they deliberate.

One committee recommended that I clean my car and desk so I could surround myself with order and begin to take control of my life. Another time, a group told me to sell my house immediately and pledged that they would welcome me at their houses for meals as I went through financial difficulties.

The several times I have called an emergency committee together, my situation rapidly came unstuck. What did it? Was it my articulation of the problem to a group of friends? The sense of accountability to a larger context? The fresh alternatives that my friends, themselves not in the stuck situation, could offer? Or was it simply their love, care, and confidence that helped me overcome my isolation?

OFTEN WHEN I THINK I've discovered a little piece of "the truth," I look a little deeper and find an opposite idea that also seems true. The stories in this chapter, and the others in this book, may have truth in them but they are not the final word. For example, I have suggested that putting pressure on one's adversary is counterproductive to the change process. But I also know that applying pressure can be both effective and appropriate. Recently I was waiting in an endless line to pay my phone bill; the problem was that there was only one clerk. I knocked on the supervisor's door and asked her to send out another clerk; she offered a flimsy excuse but did nothing. Finally, a fellow billpayer got us all yelling, "The phone company is bad! The phone company is bad!" Very soon, another clerk appeared.

Over and over I find myself saying, "I have to walk on both feet." At the International Hotel we had to act as though we expected to live there forever—fix up rooms, paint, and maintain the building—

and at the same time prepare for eviction. At Sixth Street Park we honored the street people's need to drink in peace, while at the same time looking for ways to help them out of their cycle of drinking and despair.

So I try to walk on both feet and accept paradox. And even this is incomplete. Maybe our evolutionary task is to learn to see even more complexity, to walk on three or four or ten feet, to move beyond seeing the world in dualistic terms. I try to follow my best ideas without clinging so tenaciously to them that I can't face their flaws, can't modify or discard them when appropriate. Keeping other truths in mind when acting on the truth I've chosen mitigates against fanaticism and gives balance and power to my actions.

The most difficult paradox to hold, and perhaps the most important, is imbedded in the thorny question: Can my actions make a difference in the world? Most of us cling to either a "yes" or a "no" answer, fearing that the opposite may be true. In moments of clarity I see truth in both responses. Of course my actions make a difference! And it's preposterous that my actions could make a difference!

In one sense, history is ours and we are making it all the time, through what we do and what we don't do. Ordinary people have made a difference in the history of the world, and I count myself among them.

Since the International Hotel campaign, the matter of residential hotels for poor people has never been the same in San Francisco. The other day I read in the paper that tenants in a residential hotel in Chinatown had won a bid to buy their hotel through their rent. The I-Hotel campaign helped lay the groundwork for that victory, and my work played a part in that.

On the banks of the Ganga, a sewage treatment plant will be built soon, and people in India are changing their consciousness about their river. My work and encouragement has helped this campaign along.

Surely the nuclear comedy field has been enriched by my work. Can we measure the success by the quantity of laughter? In the work against nuclear war, it's particularly hard to have much sense of accomplishment, but I always remember my friend Bob's story. In a taxicab in New York City, the driver asked him what his work was. Bob said, "I'm working to prevent nuclear war." "You're doing a great job," the driver replied. "Keep up the good work!"

And yet isn't it a folly of the ego to think that I can make a significant difference in the world? I have worked to help poor people in this country, but on the whole their situation is getting worse; the gap between rich and poor is growing. In spite of my work against war and nuclear war, the fact remains that in all of human history there have been only three hundred years without war—and none of them in my lifetime. Dangerous new technologies and nuclear war–fighting plans are increasing the risks of nuclear war. In a real sense, the Ganga can never be cleaned fast enough; children die every day as a result of the pollution.

Although these two perspectives appear to be contradictory, I try to hold both of them in my mind. I weigh them against each other and allow both to inform me. But I act on the conviction that everyone *is* making a difference. Just by living our lives, consuming space and resources, we are making a difference. Our choice is what kind of difference to make.

Epilogue: A Letter to the People of the Future

THIS IS THE WAY it was for the ordinary people of the late twentieth century who worked to resolve the massive issues of our era. At times the inertia against us and inside us seemed overwhelming. It was very hard to feel that things were going well. We never knew whether we were numerous enough, whether we had enough good ideas and a sufficiently compelling social and spiritual vision to make a significant difference. It seemed as though we would have to work forever and even then the only thing we would know for sure was that the world hadn't blown up *yet*. Sometimes it felt as though our hearts carried so much of the world's suffering they would surely break.

181

And yet it was, in many ways, an easy and natural life. Our work brought us into contact with fine people, and the further into the forest we traveled together, the clearer the sky became and the stronger our muscles grew for the long haul.

Our alliance with you, the people of the future, became stronger and clearer. We worked on your behalf, although we don't know you. I imagine that things are not much easier for you in your world than they were for us in ours. I am sure you are working to make your world better, working against what may seem impossible odds. Maybe the work to save the rivers and the air seems as antiquated to you as the battle against smallpox seemed to us. Maybe the struggle to put war away as an instrument of policy-making has made some strides, and nuclear weapons and their dreadful successors are no longer consuming nations' economic lifeblood. Maybe, through a transformation of consciousness, people have learned to act more responsibly toward the places they inhabit and care for. And maybe people have come to understand that their individual and collective well-being is dependent upon that of everyone with whom they share the planet.

If these conditions, or even some of them, exist in your world, then in every molecule of my ashes the atoms are arranged in a smile. I helped nurture these changes, and I am thankful for all the effort of the others who tended these fragile changes and allowed them to flower.

Take heart, people of the future, from our times when prospects seemed so bleak and frightening. I am sure there are aspects of life in your time and place which are equally difficult. Are you still working to redistribute the world's resources, so that the poor have more? Are you struggling to develop a new economic order where the employer/employee system is replaced by cooperatives run by worker-owners? What are your other challenges? It's difficult for me to imagine. I know your goals may appear impossible to attain. But remember all the changes that have already occurred. In every period of history, people have fought against impossible odds. Some have made it; some haven't. But I wish you well. To have made it this far, human beings in your time must already possess a greater sense of connectedness than we did.

Work for all of us who went before you. Develop an analysis of what is happening, and look for the best ideas. Fight your tendency to avoid pain and suffering. Accept your fears, be informed by them, and learn how to set them aside. Develop an even deeper connection to the creatures you share the planet with. Enjoy the absurdity around you. And remember: We put a lot of effort into making your life on this planet possible, so don't let us down.

How I wish I knew now what the ideas and challenges of your time are. I imagine it would make my task in the 1980s easier. How I almost envy you, knowing the human species made it past the eighties, into the twenty-first century, and beyond.

How We Wrote This Book

Heart Politics is the fruit of a collaborative process. For years friends had been telling me that I should write a book of all the stories they'd heard me tell. This sounded like a great idea, except I had no idea how to write a book, and I have always found living my life more interesting than digesting it. But finally, in 1980, my friend Linda Hess began interviewing me for this book, taping stories and then transcribing them. When she became consumed with other work, my comedy partner Charlie agreed to take over. (Offstage, he is a freelance writer and editor.) Later, our friend Myra—who was already working with us as censor and road manager of our comedy show—joined the project. Linda stayed on as advisor and final text editor.

Early on, Charlie started needling me to do some writing myself. He was a good coach and cheerleader, and I soon began a morning writing regimen. Dr. James Finn, my mentor at USC, had always encouraged his students to write. His advice was: Get up early in the morning and write for two hours, whether or not you have anything to say. So I tried this approach. No matter where I was, in San Francisco or Varanasi or somewhere in between, I would write. It was like playing a slot machine. Every morning I would put my nickel in and see what rolled out—stories of my work, random thoughts on social change or my philosophy of life. Charlie periodically scrounged around my desk and removed my writings before they got lost. The quality, he reported, fluctuated wildly. But he always had something encouraging to say.

Doc Finn had also suggested that we end our day's writing in the middle of a sentence, so we could later pick up where we'd left off. But I found the new day always brought new ideas, so I never did bother to pick up where I had left off. Charlie and Myra found my half-finished sentences maddening.

After a while, the files filled a large cardboard box; it was time to separate the important ideas from the meanderings and get them into some order. In this task I was absolutely at sea, but Myra and Charlie came through. They read through thick files of tape transcripts and my daily contributions, cutting and pasting, trying to organize the pieces into a sequence that was chronological or at least logical.

Myra proved to be particularly adept at recognizing valuable information: culling the few grains of wheat from the mountains of chaff, designing a structure for the book and for each chapter, identifying the stories and concepts that needed further exploration. Charlie churned out drafts of chapters, writing and rewriting until we had something we liked.

To focus our attention on the book, we went on periodic retreats. (Later we called them "advances," a term that seemed more accurate.) We were surprised how much we enjoyed this concentrated workstyle. Charlie and I would sit at opposite ends of a sundeck, each with our electric typewriter on a long extension cord. Myra moved back and forth between our stations, assigning us new jobs and keeping us on track. She called the process "dueling typewriters."

With each advance, we grew more immersed in the project. My

dreams began to reflect the day's book discussions. Myra and Charlie often found themselves sitting in bed late at night discussing the power of context or trying to figure out the most appropriate metaphor for Sixth Street Park. On comedy tours, driving from one town to another, we would schedule in time to thrash out particular concepts.

In the fall of 1983, when we had completed drafts of the first few chapters, we sent them out for comments and criticisms to twenty "test readers." We selected some people familiar with me and my stories, as well as some for whom they would be totally new. Their comments encouraged us to go on, forced us to sharpen our thinking, and helped us plan our next steps.

Around the same time, we formalized our partnership as Peavey, Levy, and Varon (a nonprophet social change work group), and held our first annual brunch for about forty friends and supporters. We reported on the progress of the manuscript and our plan to finish it within a year. This was a leap—we were sharing "ownership" of the book with a wider group, and making ourselves accountable to them.

In the intense period of work that followed, we called upon members of this community over and over. They helped sustain us financially, so that we could take the time to finish the project. When Charlie's typewriter died, and we decided finally to get a computer, friends and supporters helped us raise money to buy one. We also turned to our community for help in shaping our ideas, and several were instrumental in forcing us to probe deeper in the chapters on war, the environment, and context.

Writing the last four chapters of the book proved to be our most challenging task. Myra insisted that my thoughts on social change must have come from somewhere, and she set out to find where they came from and how I had tested them. The three of us would sit around the typewriter, and later around the computer. Myra would interview me, trying to steer the discussion in the most productive direction. Gazing out the window, I would search for the origins of my ideas. Charlie would prod me on, celebrating the victories and racing to keep up on the typewriter.

Myra drew a series of large charts, with each idea represented in a little bubble. We'd tape the charts to a wall and stare up at them, trying to find themes that united the bubbles and could become chapters. We used marking pens to color–code groups of ideas, and for months, before we had names or numbers for the chapters, we referred to them by color. Again, we sent drafts of chapters to readers from New Hampshire to Vancouver, and again we revised.

Collaborating is never entirely smooth or easy, and frankly we've had our wars and skirmishes—most of them blessedly short. The searching and rethinking that came about in the process of these conflicts have made this a stronger book. Most of our disagreements focused on whether to omit particular stories or concepts. For instance, I insisted that we include in Chapter 12 the following sentence: "Connectedness is instrumental in the release of both actomorphs (those great chemicals which move the activist muscles of the body) and their enzyme cousins, involvomorphs." Among our sample readers, there was some controversy about this sentence, and to my sadness Myra and Charlie deleted it.

As the book neared completion, Charlie and Myra met every week with Linda, poring over drafts, fine-tuning the manuscript chapter by chapter. My job during these meetings was to take care of Linda's three-year-old daughter Karuna—listening to meditative music, playing with makeup, and gathering eggs from the chickens in my backyard. My work on the manuscript was largely finished, and I was starting to get restless, tired of living in the past. Yet I knew that all the reviewing and reflection had forced me to confront new questions and had deepened my thinking.

I want to stress that no conclusion in this book is cast in concrete. I expect my ideas to change, my understanding to deepen with new information and experience. I am looking forward to the dialogue that the ideas in this book may encourage and am eager to know your thoughts. Please feel free to contact us through New Society Publishers.

Many owners share this body, says Kabir, the fifteenth-century Hindi poet. And many people share credit for the appearance of this book. Our gratitude goes first of all to Linda Hess, who does not abandon manuscripts.

Leonard Rifas, in addition to being one of our most reliable and helpful critics, drew the illustrations with patience and good humor.

Emily Levy and Jan Thomas provided us with invaluable criticism and direction, reading an endless stream of drafts and revisions, and staying on call during the most pressured periods.

Special thanks, too, to all of our test readers: Charlie Adams, Rita Archibald, Katy Butler, Paul Clements, Fred Cook, Nancy Davis, Bob Fuller and Alia Johnson, Annette Goodheart, Jan Hartsough, David Hoffman and Sharon Nelson, Jeff Howard, Sandy Kalmakoff, Jaques Kaswan, Margo King and John Steiner, Ann Kreilkamp, Rosa Lane and Margaret Pavel, Mort Levy, Jeanne Lohmann, Joanna Macy, Karen Mercer, Michael Phillips, Ray Raphael, Wilbur Rehmann, Carol Rothman, Ann Shankland, Starhawk, Diane Thomas, Janet Varon, Maurice and Zipporah Varon, and Lezlie Wagman.

From fact-checking to funding to moral support, and for a myriad other kinds of support, we thank, Shepherd Bliss, Ted Braude and Vicki Yelletz, John Burks, David Caggiano, Bruce Cook, Emil DeGuzman, Betty, Joel, and John Devalcourt, Andora Freeman, David and Peter Hartsough, Joe Havens, Barbara Hazard, Michel Henry, Gene Knudsen-Hoffman, Nan Hohenstein, Marlow Hotchkiss and Cynthia Jurs, Lyn Hurwich, Michael Katz, Vicky Lee, Barbara and Michael Levy, Phyllis Lyon and Del Martin, Joshua Mailman, Emily Mehling, Evelyn Messinger and Kim Spencer, S.K. Mishra, V.B. Mishra, Ben Morales-Correa, Arthur O'Donnell, Brad Paul, Kathleen Paulo, Lu and Wendell Phillips, Bev Ramsay, Nancy Ramsey, Kaz Tanahashi, Milton Taubman, Mark Tilsen, Ann Tompkins, S.N. Upadhyay, Bill Wahpepah, Liz Walker, Helen Waterford, Viola Weinberg, Susan Wells, John White, Claude Whitmyer, the folks at Capp Street Foundation, particularly Jane Fischberg, the students of the University of Wisconsin program in Varanasi, the reference librarians of the San Francisco Public Library and of the Meiklejohn Civil Liberties Library, and the people who attended the first heart politics talks and workshops in Montana and Massachusetts.

Thanks to the folks at New Society Publishers—David Albert, Matt Becker, Nina Huizinga, and Ellen Sawislak—whose persistence, commitment, and hard work helped bring you this book.

Finally, I would like to express my deepest gratitude to Charlie and Myra, who worked so hard to understand and who have so faithfully presented the ideas in this book. That we have had great fun and remain good friends in the process of birthing Heart Politics is a real miracle. And considering how closely we have worked together on every detail, the fact that I have sneaked this thank-you into the book without their knowing is also something of a miracle. Surprise, Myra and Charlie! Friends and partners, you have contributed immeasurably to the development of my thinking.

References

Chapter 2/SEEDS
The quotation from Chief Joseph is taken from Merrill D. Beal's *"I Will Fight No More Forever": Chief Joseph and the Nez Perce War* (Seattle: University of Washington Press, 1966), page 229.

Chapter 7/WOULD YOU DO THIS TO YOUR MOTHER?
Russell Means's speech was published as "Fighting Words on the Future of the Earth," in *Mother Jones*, December 1980, pages 22–38.
Some of the information and quoted matter on the Minamata victims' campaign is drawn from the book *Minamata* by W. Eugene and Aileen M. Smith (New York: Holt, Rinehart & Winston, 1975).

Chapter 10/THE POWER OF CONTEXT
The quotation from Stewart Brand that precedes this chapter is from an unpublished "Destination Crisis" paper written in 1971. Myra unearthed it one afternoon in the offices of the *Whole Earth Review* in Sausalito, California.

Chapter 11/US AND THEM
The Saul Alinsky quotation is from his *Rules for Radicals* (New York: Vintage Books, 1972), page 134.

Chapter 12/OBSTACLES TO CHANGE
Amplification of Everett Rogers' ideas can be found in his *Diffusion of Innovations* (New York: Free Press, 1983).
The quotations from Bob Fuller are from "A Better Game than War: Interviews with Robert Fuller," *Evolutionary Blues* #2, Spring

1983, pages 19 and 20. (Available from P.O. Box 4448, Arcata, CA 95521.)

Chapter 13/TALES OF CHANGE

The retelling of the Shambhala prophecy is adapted from an interview with Joanna Macy in *Yoga Journal*, January/February 1985, pages 46 and 51.

Deborah Lubar's listening story is taken from her article "Breath" in *Humpty Dumpty Report* #6, August/September 1983, pages 11–15. (Available from P.O. Box 4742, Berkeley, CA 94704.)

The oral history of C.P. Ellis appears in Studs Terkel's *American Dreams: Lost and Found* (New York: Ballantine, 1981), pages 221–233.

For more on Stanley Milgram's research, see his *Obedience and Authority* (New York: Harper & Row, 1974).

More Resources From
New Society Publishers

This Way Daybreak Comes: Women's Values and the Future

by Annie Cheatham and Mary Clare Powell
Foreword by Gloria Anzaldúa co-editor of *This Bridge Called My Back: Writings by Radical Women of Color*

280 pages. Illustrated. Photographs. Appendices. Index. 1986.
Paper $12.95
Cloth $34.95

Take Off the Masks

by Malcolm Boxd
foreword by Harry Britt, Board of Supervisors, City and County of San Francisco.

200 pages. 1984.
Paper $7.95
Cloth$24.95

Despair and Personal Power in the Nuclear Age

by Joanna Rogers Macy

Appendices, resource lists, exercises. Large format. 200 pages. 1983.

More Than The Troubles: A Common Sense Vie of the Northern Ireland Conflict
  by Lynne Shivers and David Bowman, S.J.
  Foreword by Denis Barntt
  Appendix by Joseph Fahey on "Northern Ireland: Its Relevance for Peace Education"

  240 pages. Index. Appendices. Maps. Charts. Bibliographies. Photographs.

Our Stunning Harvest: Poems by Ellen Bass

  Foreword by Florence Howe

  Paper $6.96
  Cloth $19.95

Nonviolent Struggle in the Middle East

  by R. Scott Kennedy and Mubarak E. Awad
  Foreword by David H. Albert

  Contains two essays: *The Druze of the Golan: A Case of Nonviolent Resistance* and *Nonviolent Resistance: A Strategy for the Occupied Territories.*

  40 pages. 1985.
  Staplebound $2.95

Bearing Witness, Building Bridges: Interviews with North Americans Living and Working in Nicaragua

  edited with an Introduction by Melissa Everett
  Photographs by Michael Kopec
  Foreword by Congressman Bruce Morrison
  Afterword by Sr. Marjorie Tuite, Church United

  200 pages. Photographs. Appendices.
  Paper $8.95
  Cloth $29.95

To order, send check to:
New Society Publishers
4722 Baltimore Avenue
Philadelphia, PA 19143

For postage and handling:
Add $1.50 for first publication. 40¢ for each additional.

Write for our complete literature list.